The World's Famous Orations

VOL. VI

IRELAND

1775—1902

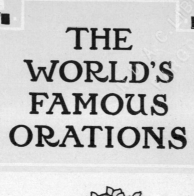

THE WORLD'S FAMOUS ORATIONS

WILLIAM JENNINGS BRYAN

EDITOR-IN-CHIEF

FRANCIS W. HALSEY

ASSOCIATE EDITOR

IN TEN VOLUMES

Vol. VI

IRELAND

44629

FUNK and WAGNALLS COMPANY

New York and London

CONTENTS

Vol. VI—Ireland (1775—1902)

	Page
Burke—I On Conciliation with America (1775)	3
II Principles in Politics (1780)	40
III At the Trial of Warren Hastings (1788)	50
Grattan—I A Plea for Irish Legislative Independence (1780)	59
II Invective Against Corry (1800)	71
Sheridan—At the Trial of Warren Hastings (1788)	77
Curran—I In Behalf of Rowan and Free Speech (1794)	99
II At the Prosecution of Johnson for Libel (1805)	127
Wolf Tone—On Being Found Guilty (1798)	132
Emmet—On Being Found Guilty of Treason (1803)	137
Charles Phillips—I An Address to Catholics	149
II The Character of Napoleon (About 1817)	157
Lord Plunket—On Catholic Relief (1821)	162
Sheil—I On the Irish as "Aliens" (1837)	173
II On the Disabilities of the Jews (1848)	177

44629

CONTENTS

Page

ISAAC BUTT—At the Bar of the House of Lords
(1840) 188

O'CONNELL—In Favor of the Repeal of the Union (1843) 195

MEAGHER—On Abhorring the Sword (1846) . 209

A. M. SULLIVAN—On the Zulu War (1879) . 217

PARNELL—I On the Forged Letter Printed in
the London *Times* (1887) 224

II On the Home Rule Bill (1888) . . . 230

MICHAEL DAVITT—On the Irish Land League
(1889) 244

JOHN DILLON—On the Death of Gladstone
(1898) 253

JOHN E. REDMOND—Ireland and the Coronation
(1902) 256

VOL. VI
IRELAND
1775—1902

BURKE

I

ON CONCILIATION WITH AMERICA[1]

(1775)

Born in 1729, died in 1797; elected to Parliament in 1766; Privy Councilor in 1782; conducted the impeachment of Warren Hastings in 1787-95, having resigned his seat in Parliament.

WE are called upon again to attend to America; to attend to the whole of it together; and to review the subject with an unusual degree of care and calmness.

Surely it is an awful subject, or there is none so on this side of the grave. When I first had the honor of a seat in this House, the affairs of that continent pressed themselves upon us as the most important and most delicate object of parliamentary attention. My little share in this great deliberation oppressed me. I found myself a partaker in a very high trust; and having no sort of reason to rely on the strength of my natural abilities for the proper execution of that

---

[1] Delivered in the House of Commons, March 22, 1775, in support of thirteen resolutions looking to conciliation. Abridged. Burke spoke for three hours. Mackintosh describes this speech as "the most faultless of Mr. Burke's productions." The resolutions were lost by a vote of 270 to 78. When the result became known in America, the "embattled farmers" had already met the British at Concord Bridge.

trust, I was obliged to take more than common pains to instruct myself in everything which relates to our Colonies. I was not less under the necessity of forming some fixed ideas concerning the general policy of the British Empire. Something of this sort seemed to be indispensable, in order, amid so vast a fluctuation of passions and opinions, to concenter my thoughts; to ballast my conduct; to preserve me from being blown about by every wind of fashionable doctrine. I really did not think it safe or manly to have fresh principles to seek upon every fresh mail which should arrive from America.

At that period I had the fortune to find myself in perfect concurrence with a large majority in this House.[1] Bowing under that high authority, and penetrated with the sharpness and strength of that early impression, I have continued ever since in my original sentiments without the least deviation. Whether this be owing to an obstinate perseverance in error, or to a religious adherence to what appears to me truth and reason, it is in your equity to judge.

To restore order and repose to an Empire so great and so distracted as ours, is merely in the attempt an undertaking that would ennoble the flights of the highest genius, and obtain pardon for the efforts of the meanest understanding. Struggling a good while with these thoughts,

[1] Burke refers here to the repeal of the Stamp Act, when the vote was 276 to 161.

by degrees I felt myself more firm. I derived, at length, some confidence from what in other circumstances usually produces timidity. I grew less anxious, even from the idea of my own insignificance. For, judging of what you are by what you ought to be, I persuaded myself that you would not reject a reasonable proposition because it had nothing but its reason to recommend it. On the other hand, being totally destitute of all shadow of influence, natural or adventitious, I was very sure that if my proposition were futile or dangerous—if it were weakly conceived or improperly timed, there was nothing exterior to it of power to awe, dazzle, or delude you. You will see it just as it is, and you will treat it just as it deserves.

The PROPOSITION is peace. Not peace through the medium of war, not peace to be hunted through the labyrinth of intricate and endless negotiations; not peace to arise out of universal discord, fomented from principle, in all parts of the Empire; not peace to depend on the juridical determination of perplexing questions, or the precise marking the shadowy boundaries of a complex government. It is simple peace, sought in its natural course and its ordinary haunts. It is peace sought in the spirit of peace, and laid in principles purely pacific. I propose, by removing the ground of the difference, and by restoring *the former unsuspecting confidence of the Colonies in the mother country*, to give permanent satisfaction to your people;

and, far from a scheme of ruling by discord, to reconcile them to each other in the same act, and by the bond of the very same interest, which reconciles them to British government.

My idea is nothing more. Refined policy ever has been the parent of confusion, and ever will be so long as the world endures. Plain good intention, which is as easily discovered at the first view as fraud is surely detected at last, is (let me say) of no mean force in the government of mankind. Genuine simplicity of heart is a healing and cementing principle. My plan, therefore, being formed upon the most simple grounds imaginable, may disappoint some people when they hear it. It has nothing to recommend it to the pruriency of curious ears. There is nothing at all new and captivating in it. It has nothing of the splendor of the project which has been lately laid upon your table by the noble lord in the blue ribbon.[1] It does not propose to fill your lobby with squabbling colony agents, who will require the interposition of your mace at every instant to keep the peace among them. It does not institute a magnificent auction of finance, where captivated provinces come to general ransom by bidding against each

---

[1] Lord North, who on February 20 of this year had carried a resolution that so long as the Colonies taxed themselves with the consent of the king and Parliament, no other taxes should be imposed. Gibbon heard the spirited debate which the resolution evoked, and has described it graphically in a letter to his friend Holroyd.

other, until you knock down the hammer, and determine a proportion of payments beyond all the powers of algebra to equalize and settle.

The capital leading questions on which you must this day decide, are these two: *First, whether you ought to concede; and, secondly, what your concession ought to be.*

On the first of these questions we have gained, as I have just taken the liberty of observing to you, some ground. But I am sensible that a good deal more is still to be done. Indeed, sir, to enable us to determine both on the one and the other of these great questions with a firm and precise judgment, I think it may be necessary to consider distinctly the true nature and the peculiar *circumstances* of the object which we have before us; because, after all our struggle, whether we will or not, we must govern America according to that nature and to those circumstances, and not according to our imaginations; not according to abstract ideas of right; by no means according to mere general theories of government, the resort to which appears to me, in our present situation, no better than arrant trifling. I shall therefore endeavor, with your leave, to lay before you some of the most material of these circumstances in as full and as clear a manner as I am able to state them.

The first thing that we have to consider with regard to the nature of the object, is the number of people in the Colonies. I have taken for some years a good deal of pains on that point. I can by no calculation justify myself in placing the number below two millions of inhabitants of our own European blood and color, besides at least five hundred thousand others, who form no inconsiderable part of the strength and opulence of the whole. This, sir, is, I believe, about the true number. There is no occasion to exaggerate, where plain truth is of so much weight and importance. But whether I put the present numbers too high or too low, is a matter of little moment. Such is the strength with which population shoots in that part of the world, that, state the numbers as high as we will, while the dispute continues, the exaggeration ends. While we are discussing any given magnitude, they are grown to it. While we spend our time in deliberating on the mode of governing two millions, we shall find we have two millions more to manage. Your children do not grow faster from infancy to manhood, than they spread from families to communities, and from villages to nations.

I put this consideration of the present and the growing numbers in the front of our deliberation; because, sir, this consideration will make it evident to a blunter discernment than yours, that no partial, narrow, contracted, pinched, occasional system will be at all suitable to such an object. It will show you that it is not to be considered as one of those *minima* which are out of the eye and consideration of the law; not a paltry excrescence of the State; not a mean dependent, who may be neglected with little damage, and provoked with little danger. It will prove that some degree of care and caution is required in the handling of such an object; it will show that you ought not, in reason, to trifle with so large a mass of the interests and feelings of the human race. You could at no time do so without guilt; and, be assured, you will not do it long with impunity.

I have in my hand two accounts: one a comparative state of the export trade of England to its Colonies as it stood in the year 1704, and as it stood in the year 1772; the other a state of the export trade of this country to its Colonies alone, as it stood in 1772, compared with the whole trade of England to all parts of the world, the Colonies included, in the year 1704. They are from good vouchers; the latter period from the accounts on your table, the earlier from an original manuscript of Davenant, who first established the inspector-general's office, which has been ever since his time so abundant a source of parliamentary information.

The trade to the Colonies, taken on the export side, at the beginning of this century, that is, in the year 1704, stood thus:

Exports to North America and the
  West Indies £483,265
To Africa   86,665
                                     _____
                                     £569,930

In the year 1772, which I take as a middle year between the highest and lowest of those lately laid on your table, the account was as follows:

To North America and the West Indies	£4,791,734
To Africa	866,398
To which, if you add the export trade from Scotland, which had in 1704 no existence	364,000
	£6,022,132

From five hundred and odd thousand, it has grown to six millions. It has increased no less than twelvefold. This is the state of the Colony trade, as compared with itself at these two periods, within this century; and this is matter for meditation. But this is not all. Examine my second account. See how the export trade to the Colonies alone in 1772 stood in the other point of view, that is, as compared to the whole trade of England in 1704.

The whole export trade of England, including that to the Colonies, in 1704	£6,509,000
Exported to the Colonies alone, in 1772	6,024,000
Difference .	£485,000

The trade with America alone is now within less than £500,000 of being equal to what this great commercial nation, England, carried on at the beginning of this century with the whole world! If I had taken the largest year of those on your table, it would rather have exceeded.

But, it will be said, is not this American trade an unnatural protuberance, that has drawn the juices from the rest of the body? The reverse. It is the very food that has nourished every other part into its present magnitude. Our general trade has been greatly augmented, and augmented more or less in almost every part to which it ever extended, but with this material difference, that of the six millions in which in the beginning of the century constituted the whole mass of our export commerce, the colony trade was but one-twelfth part; it is now (as a part of sixteen millions) considerably more than a third of the whole. This is the relative proportion of the importance of the Colonies of these two periods; and all reasoning concerning our mode of treating them must have this proportion as its basis, or it is a reasoning weak, rotten, and sophistical.

Mr. Speaker, I can not prevail on myself to hurry over this great consideration. It is good for us to be here. We stand where we have an immense view of what is, and what is past. Clouds, indeed, and darkness, rest upon the future. Let us, however, before we descend from this noble eminence, reflect that this growth of our national prosperity has happened within the short period of the life of man. It has happened within sixty-eight years. There are those alive whose memory might touch the two extremities. For instance, my Lord Bathurst might remember all the stages of the progress. He was in 1704 of an age at least to be made to comprehend such things.[1] He was then old enough *"acta parentum jam legere et quae sit poterit cognoscere virtus."* Suppose, sir, that the angel of this auspicious youth, foreseeing the many virtues which made him one of the most amiable, as he is one of the most fortunate men of his age,[2] had opened to him in vision, that when, in the fourth generation, the third prince of the House of Brunswick had sat twelve years on the throne of that nation, which, by the happy issue of moderate and healing councils, was to be made Great Britain, he should see his son,[3] lord chancellor of England, turn back the current of hereditary dignity to its fountain, and raise him to a higher rank of peerage, while he enriched the family with a new one. If, amid these bright and happy scenes of domestic honor and prosperity, that angel should have drawn up the curtain, and unfolded the rising glories of his

[1] Lord Bathurst was born in 1684. He died a few months after the date of Burke's speech, September 16, 1775, when in his ninety-first year.

[2] George III. at his accession granted to Lord Bathurst a pension of £2,000 a year, and in 1772 made him an earl.

[3] Henry, second Earl Bathurst, "to the surprise of the world," was made lord chancellor, January 23, 1771.

country, and while he was gazing with admiration on the then commercial grandeur of England, the genius should point out to him a little speck, scarce visible in the mass of the national interest, a small seminal principle rather than a formed body, and should tell him:

"Young man, there is America—which at this day serves for little more than to amuse you with stories of savage men and uncouth manners; yet shall, before you taste death, show itself equal to the whole of that commerce which now attracts the envy of the world. Whatever England has been growing to by a progressive increase of improvement, brought in by varieties of people, by succession of civilizing conquests and civilizing settlements in a series of seventeen hundred years you shall see as much added to her by America in the course of a single life."

If this state of his country had been foretold to him, would it not require all the sanguine credulity of youth, and all the fervid glow of enthusiasm, to make him believe it? Fortunate man, he has lived to see it! Fortunate indeed, if he lived to see nothing to vary the prospect and cloud the setting of his day!

Excuse me, sir, if turning from such thoughts, I resume this comparative view once more. You have seen it on a large scale; look at it on a small one. I will point out to your attention a particular instance of it in the single province of Pennslyvania. In the year 1704 that province called for £11,459 in value of your commodities, native and foreign. This was the whole. What did it demand in 1772? Why nearly fifty times as much; for in that year the export to Pennsylvania was £507,909, nearly equal to the export to all the Colonies together in the first period.

I choose, sir, to enter into these minute and particular details, because generalities, which, in all other cases are apt to heighten and raise the subject, have here a tendency to sink it. When we speak of the commerce with our Colonies, fiction lags after truth; invention is unfruitful, and imagination cold and barren.

I pass to the Colonies in another point of view —their agriculture. This they have prosecuted with such a spirit, that, besides feeding plentifully their own growing multitude, their annual export of grain, comprehending rice, has, some years ago, exceeded a million in value. Of their last harvest I am persuaded they will export much more. At the beginning of the century, some of these Colonies imported corn from the mother country. For some time past the old world has been fed from the new. The scarcity which you have felt would have been a desolating famine, if this child of your old age, with a true filial piety, with a Roman charity, had not put the full breast of its youthful exuberance to the mouth of its exhausted parent.

As to the wealth which the Colonies have drawn from the sea by their fisheries, you had all that matter fully opened at your bar. You surely thought those acquisitions of value, for they seemed even to excite your envy; and yet, the spirit by which that enterprising employment has been exercised, ought rather, in my opinion, to have raised your esteem and admiration. And pray, sir, what in the world is equal to it? Pass by the other parts, and look at the manner in which the people of New England have of late carried on the whale fishery. While we follow them among the tumbling mountains of ice, and behold them penetrating into the deepest frozen recesses of Hudson's Bay and Davis' Straits—while we are looking for them beneath the arctic circle, we hear that they have pierced into the opposite region of polar cold—that they are at the antipodes, and engaged under the frozen Serpent of the south. Falkland Island, which seemed too remote and romantic an object for the grasp of national ambition, is but a stage and resting-place in the progress of their victorious industry.

Nor is the equinoctial heat more discouraging to them than the accumulated winter of both the poles. We know that while some of them draw the line, and strike the harpoon on the coast of Africa, others run the longitude, and pursue their gigantic game along the coast of Brazil. No sea but what is vexed by their fisheries. No climate that is not witness to their toils. Neither the perseverance of Holland, nor the activity of France, nor the dexterous and firm sagacity of English enterprise, ever carried this most perilous mode of hardy industry to the extent to which it has been pushed by this recent people—a people who are still, as it were, but in the gristle, and not yet hardened into the bone of manhood. When I contemplate these things—when I know that the Colonies in general owe little or nothing to any care of ours, and that they are not squeezed into this happy form by the constraints of watchful and suspicious government, but that, through a wise and salutary neglect, a generous nature has been suffered to take her own way to perfection—when I reflect upon these effects—when I see how profitable they have been to us, I feel all the pride of power sink, and all presumption in the wisdom of human contrivances melt and die away within me. My rigor relents. I pardon something to the spirit of liberty.

I am sensible, sir, that all which I have asserted in my detail is admitted in the gross; but that quite a different conclusion is drawn from it. America, gentlemen say, is a noble object. It is an object well worth fighting for. Certainly it is, if fighting a people be the best way of gaining them.

First, sir, permit me to observe, that the use of force alone is but *temporary*. It may subdue for a moment, but it does not remove the necessity of subduing again; and a nation is not governed which is perpetually to be conquered.

My next objection is its *uncertainty*. Terror is not always the effect of force; and an armament is not a victory. If you do not succeed, you are without resource; for, conciliation failing, force remains; but, force failing, no further hope of reconciliation is left. Power and authority are sometimes bought by kindness but they can never be begged as alms by an impoverished and defeated violence.

A further objection to force is, that you *impair the object* by your very endeavors to preserve it. The thing you fought for is not the thing which you recover; but depreciated, sunk, wasted, and consumed in the contest. Nothing less will content me than *whole* America. I do not choose to consume its strength along with our own, because in all parts it is the British strength that I consume. I do not choose to be caught by a foreign enemy at the end of this exhausting conflict, and still less in the midst of it.[1] I may escape; but I can make no insurance against such an event. Let me add, that I do not choose wholly to break the American spirit, because it is the spirit that has made the country.

These, sir, are my reasons for not entertaining that high opinion of untried force, by which many gentlemen, for whose sentiments in other particulars I have great respect, seem to be so greatly captivated.

But there is still behind a third consideration concerning this object, which serves to determine

[1] The alliance with France was secured by the Colonies "in the midst of it"—that is, after the defeat of Burgoyne in October, 1777,

my opinion on the sort of policy which ought to be pursued in the management of America, even more than its population and its commerce —I mean its temper and character. In this character of the Americans *a love of freedom* is the predominating feature, which marks and distinguishes the whole; and, as an ardent is always a jealous affection, your Colonies become suspicious, restive, and untractable, whenever they see the least attempt to wrest from them by force, or shuffle from them by chicane, what they think the only advantage worth living for. This fierce spirit of liberty is stronger in the English Colonies, probably, than in any other people of the earth, and this from a variety of powerful causes, which, to understand the true temper of their minds, and the direction which this spirit takes, it will not be amiss to lay open somewhat more largely.

First, the people of the Colonies are descendants of Englishmen. England, sir, is a nation which still, I hope, respects, and formerly adored her freedom. The Colonists emigrated from you when this part of your character was most predominant[1]; and they took this bias and direction the moment they parted from your hands. They are, therefore, not only devoted to liberty, but to liberty according to English ideas and on English principles. Abstract liberty, like other mere

[1] That is, during the Parliamentary struggles with Charles I. and James II., when in New England, New York, Pennsylvania, and Virginia English Colonies were planted.

abstractions, is not to be found. Liberty inheres in some sensible object; and every nation has formed to itself some favorite point which, by way of eminence, becomes the criterion of their happiness. It happened, you know, sir, that the great contests for freedom in this country were, from the earliest times chiefly upon the question of taxing.

Religion, always a principle of energy, in this new people is no way worn out or impaired; and their mode of professing it is also one main cause of this free spirit. The people are Protestants; and of that kind which is the most averse to all implicit submission of mind and opinion. This is a persuasion not only favorable to liberty, but built upon it. I do not think, sir, that the reason of this averseness in the dissenting churches from all that looks like absolute government, is so much to be sought in their religious tenets, as in their history. Everyone knows that the Roman Catholic religion is at least coeval with most of the governments where it prevails; that it has generally gone hand in hand with them; and received great favor and every kind of support from authority. The Church of England, too, was formed from her cradle under the nursing care of regular government. But the dissenting interests have sprung up in direct opposition to all the ordinary powers of the world, and could justify that opposition only on a strong claim to natural liberty. Their very existence depended on the powerful and un-remitted assertion of that claim. All Protestantism, even the most cold and passive, is a kind of dissent.

But the religion most prevalent in our northern Colonies is a refinement on the principle of resistance; it is the dissidence of dissent and the Protestantism of the Protestant religion. This religion, under a variety of denominations, agreeing in nothing but in the communion of the spirit of liberty, is predominant in most of the northern Provinces, where the Church of England, notwithstanding its legal rights, is in reality no more than a sort of private sect, not composing, most probably, the tenth of the people.

Sir, I can perceive by their manner that some gentlemen object to the latitude of this description, because in the southern Colonies the Church of England forms a large body, and has a regular establishment. It is certainly true. There is, however, a circumstance attending these Colonies, which, in my opinion, fully counterbalances this difference, and makes the spirit of liberty still more high and haughty than in those to the northward. It is that in Virginia and the Carolinas they have a vast multitude of *slaves*. Where this is the case in any part of the world, those who are free are by far the most proud and jealous of their freedom. Freedom is to them not only an enjoyment, but a kind of rank and privilege. Not seeing there that freedom, as in countries where it is a common blessing, and as broad and general as the air, may be united with much abject toil, with great misery, with all the exterior of servitude, liberty looks, among them, like something that is more noble and liberal. I do not mean, sir, to command the superior morality of this sentiment, which has at least as much pride as virtue in it; but I can not alter the nature of man. The fact is so; and these people of the southern Colonies are much more strongly, and with a higher and more stubborn spirit, attached to liberty than those to the northward. Such were all the ancient commonwealths; such were our Gothic ancestors; such, in our days, were the Poles, and such will be all masters of slaves, who are not slaves themselves. In such a people the haughtiness of domination combines with the spirit of freedom, fortifies it, and renders it invincible.

Permit me, sir, to add another circumstance in our Colonies, which contributes no mean part toward the growth and effect of this untractable spirit—I mean their *education*. In no country perhaps in the world is the law so general a study. The profession itself is numerous and powerful; and in most provinces it takes the lead. The greater number of the deputies sent to Congress were lawyers. But all who read, and most do read, endeavor to obtain some smattering in that science. I have been told by an eminent bookseller, that in no branch of his business, after tracts of popular devotion, were so many books as those on the law exported to the Plantations. The Colonists have now fallen into the way of printing them for their own use. I hear that they have sold nearly as many of Blackstone's Commentaries in America as in England. General Gage[1] marks out this disposition very particularly in a letter on your table. He states that all the people in his government are lawyers, or smatterers in law; and that in Boston they have been enabled, by successful chicane, wholly to evade many parts of one of your capital penal constitutions. The smartness of debate will say that this knowledge ought to teach them more clearly the rights of legislature, their obligations to obedience, and the penalties of rebellion. All this is mighty well. But my honorable and learned friend[2] on the floor, who condescends to mark what I say for animadversion, will disdain that ground. He has heard, as well as I, that when great honors and great emoluments do not win over this knowledge to the service of the State, it is a formidable adversary to government. If the spirit be not tamed and broken by these happy methods, it is stubborn and litigious. *Abeunt studia in mores.*

This study renders men acute, inquisitive, dexterous, prompt in attack, ready in defense, full of resources. In other countries, the peo-

---

[1] At this time Gage was governor of Massachusetts.
[2] Lord Thurlow, then attorney-general but not yet a peer.

ple, more simple and of a less mercurial cast, judge of an ill principle in government only by an actual grievance. Here they anticipate the evil, and judge of the pressure of the grievance by the badness of the principle. They augur misgovernment at a distance, and snuff the approach of tyranny in every tainted breeze.

The last cause of this disobedient spirit in the Colonies is hardly less powerful than the rest, as it is not merely moral, but laid deep in the natural constitution of things. Three thousand miles of ocean lie between you and them. No contrivance can prevent the effect of this distance in weakening government. Seas roll and months pass between the order and the execution; and the want of a speedy explanation of a single point is enough to defeat the whole system. You have, indeed, "winged ministers" of vengeance, who carry your bolts in their pouches to the remotest verge of the sea. But there a power steps in that limits the arrogance of raging passion and furious elements, and says: "So far shalt thou go, and no farther." Who are you, that should fret and rage, and bite the chains of nature?

Then, sir, from these six capital sources of descent, of form of government, of religion in the northern Provinces, of manners in the southern, of education, of the remoteness of situation from the first mover of government—from all these causes a fierce spirit of liberty has grown up. It has grown with the growth of the people in your Colonies, and increased with the increase of their wealth; a spirit that, unhappily meeting with an exercise of power in England, which, however lawful, is not reconcilable to any ideas of liberty, much less with theirs, has kindled this flame, that is ready to consume us.

The question is not whether their spirit deserves praise or blame. What, in the name of God, shall we do with it? You have before you the object, such as it is, with all its glories, with all its imperfections on its head. You see the magnitude, the importance, the temper, the habits, the disorders. By all these considerations we are strongly urged to determine something concerning it. We are called upon to fix some rule and line for our future conduct, which may give a little stability to our politics, and prevent the return of such unhappy deliberations as the present. Every such return will bring the matter before us in a still more untractable form. For, what astonishing and incredible things have we not seen already? What monsters have not been generated from this unnatural contention?

Sir, if I were capable of engaging you to an equal attention, I would state that, as far as I am capable of discerning, there are but three ways of proceeding relative to this stubborn spirit which prevails in your Colonies and disturbs your government. These are: to change that spirit, as inconvenient, by removing the causes; to prosecute it as criminal; or to comply with it as necessary. I would not be guilty of an imperfect enumeration. I can think of but these three. Another has, indeed, been stated— that of giving up the Colonies; but it met so slight a reception, that I do not think myself obliged to dwell a great while upon it. It is nothing but a little sally of anger, like the forwardness of peevish children, who, when they can not get all they would have, are resolved to take nothing.

The temper and character which prevail in our Colonies are, I am afraid, unalterable by any human art. We can not, I fear, falsify the pedigree of this fierce people, and persuade them that they are not sprung from a nation in whose veins the blood of freedom circulates. The language in which they would hear you tell them this tale would detect the imposition. Your speech would betray you. An Englishman is the unfittest person on earth to argue another Englishman into slavery.

I think it is nearly as little in our power to change their republican religion as their free descent; or to substitute the Roman Catholic as a penalty, or the Church of England as an improvement. The mode of inquisition and dragooning is going out of fashion in the Old World, and I should not confide much to their efficacy in the new. The education of the Americans is also on the same unalterable bottom with their religion. You can not persuade them to burn their books of curious science; to banish their lawyers from their courts of law; or to quench the lights of their assemblies, by refusing to choose those persons who are best read in their privileges. It would be no less impracticable to think of wholly annihilating the popular assemblies in which these lawyers sit. The army, by which we must govern in their place, would be far more chargeable to us; not quite so effectual; and perhaps, in the end, fully as difficult to be kept in obedience.

But let us suppose all these moral difficulties got over. The ocean remains. You can not pump this dry; and as long as it continues in its present bed, so long all the causes which weaken authority by distance will continue.

> "Ye gods! annihilate but space and time,
> And make two lovers happy!"

was a pious and passionate prayer, but just as reasonable as many of these serious wishes of very grave and solemn politicians.

If, then, sir, it seems almost desperate to think of any alternative course for changing the moral causes (and not quite easy to remove the natural) which produce the prejudices irreconcilable to the late exercise of our authority, but that the spirit infallibly will continue, and, continuing, will produce such effects as now embarrass us, the *second* mode under consideration is to prosecute that spirit in its overt acts as *criminal*.

At this proposition I must pause a moment.

The thing seems a great deal too big for my ideas of jurisprudence. It should seem, to my way of conceiving such matters, that there is a very wide difference in reason and policy between the mode of proceeding on the irregular conduct of scattered individuals, or even of bands of men, who disturb order within the State, and the civil dissensions which may, from time to time, on great questions, agitate the several communities which compose a great empire. It looks to me to be narrow and pedantic to apply the ordinary ideas of criminal justice to this great public contest. I do not know the method of drawing up an indictment against a whole people. I can not insult and ridicule the feelings of millions of my fellow creatures, as Sir Edward Coke insulted one excellent individual at the bar.[1] I am not ripe to pass sentence on the gravest public bodies, intrusted with magistracies of great authority and dignity, and charged with the safety of their fellow citizens, upon the very same title that I am. I really think that, for wise men, this is not judicious; for sober men, not decent; for minds tinctured with humanity, not mild and merciful.

Perhaps, sir, I am mistaken in my idea of an empire, as distinguished from a single state or kingdom. But my idea of it is this: that an empire is the aggregate of many states, under one common head, whether this head be a mon-

[1] Sir Walter Raleigh at his trial in 1603. Coke's conduct toward Raleigh, says one writer, "was simply infamous."

arch or a presiding republic. It does, in such constitutions, frequently happen (and nothing but the dismal, cold, dead uniformity of servitude can prevent its happening) that the subordinate parts have many local privileges and immunities. Between these privileges and the supreme common authority, the line may be extremely nice. Of course, disputes—often, too, very bitter disputes, and much ill blood, will arise. But, tho every privilege is an exemption, in the case, from the ordinary exercise of the supreme authority, it is no denial of it. The claim of a privilege seems rather, *ex vi termini*, to imply a superior power; for to talk of the privileges of a state or of a person who has no superior, is hardly any better than speaking nonsense.

Now, in such unfortunate quarrels among the component parts of a great political union of communities, I can scarcely conceive anything more completely imprudent than for the head of the Empire to insist that, if any privilege is pleaded against his will or his acts, that his *whole* authority is denied; instantly to proclaim rebellion, to beat to arms, and to put the offending Provinces under the ban. Will not this, sir, very soon teach the Provinces to make no distinctions on their part? Will it not teach them that the government against which a claim of liberty is tantamount to high treason, is a government to which submission is equivalent to slavery? It may not always be quite convenient to impress dependent communities with such an idea.

We are, indeed, in all disputes with the Colonies, by the necessity of things, the judge. It is true, sir; but I confess that the character of judge in my own cause is a thing that frightens me. Instead of filling me with pride, I am exceedingly humbled by it. I can not proceed with a stern, assured, judicial confidence, until I find myself in something more like a judicial character. I must have these hesitations as long as I am compelled to recollect that, in my little reading upon such contests as these, the sense of mankind has at least as often decided against the superior as the subordinate power. Sir, let me add, too, that the opinion of my having some abstract right in my favor would not put me much at my ease in passing sentence, unless I could be sure that there were no rights which in their exercise under certain circumstances, were not the most odious of all wrongs, and the most vexatious of all injustice. Sir, these considerations have great weight with me, when I find things so circumstanced that I see the same party at once a civil litigant against me in point of right and a culprit before me; while I sit as criminal judge on acts of his whose moral quality is to be decided on upon the merits of that very litigation. Men are every now and then put, by the complexity of human affairs, into strange situations; but justice is the same, let the judge be in what situation he will.

In this situation, let us seriously and coolly ponder. What is it we have got by all our menaces, which have been many and ferocious? What advantage have we derived from the penal laws we have passed, and which, for the time, have been severe and numerous? What advances have we made toward our object by the sending of a force which, by land and sea, is no contemptible strength? Has the disorder abated? Nothing less. When I see things in this situation, after such confident hopes, bold promises, and active exertions, I can not, for my life, avoid a suspicion that the plan itself is not correctly right.

If, then, the removal of the causes of this spirit of American liberty be, for the greater part, or rather entirely, impracticable; if the ideas of criminal process be inapplicable, or, if applicable, are in the highest degree inexpedient, what way yet remains? No way is open but the third and last—to comply with the American spirit as necessary, or, if you please, to submit to it as a necessary evil.

If we adopt this mode, if we mean to conciliate and concede, let us see, of what nature the concessions ought to be. To ascertain the nature of our concession, we must look at their complaint. The Colonies complain that they have not the characteristic mark and seal of British freedom. They complain that they are taxed in Parliament in which they are not represented. If you mean to satisfy them at all, you must satisfy them with regard to this complaint. If you mean to please any people, you must give them the boon which they ask; not what you may think better for them, but of a kind totally different. Such an act may be a wise regulation, but is no concession, whereas our present theme is the mode of giving satisfaction.

The question with me is, not whether you have a right to render your people miserable, but whether it is not your interest to make them happy. It is not what a lawyer tells me I *may* do, but what humanity, reason, and justice tell me I *ought* to do. Is a politic act the worse for being a generous one? Is no concession proper but that which is made from your want of right to keep what you grant? Or does it lessen the grace or dignity of relaxing in the exercise of an odious claim, because you have your evidence-room full of titles, and your magazines stuffed with arms to enforce them?

Such is steadfastly my opinion of the absolute necessity of keeping up the concord of this Empire by a unity of spirit, tho in a diversity of operations, that, if I were sure the Colonists had, at their leaving this country, sealed a regular compact of servitude; that they had solemnly abjured all the rights of citizens; that they had made a vow to renounce all ideas of liberty for them and their posterity to all generations, yet I should hold myself obliged to conform to the temper I found universally prevalent in my own day, and to govern two millions of men, impa-

tient of servitude, on the principles of freedom.
I am not determining a point of law. I am restoring tranquillity, and the general character
and situation of a people must determine what
sort of government is fitted for them. That
point nothing else can or ought to determine.

My idea, therefore, without considering
whether we yield as matter of right, or grant
as matter of favor, is *to admit the people of our
Colonies into an interest in the Constitution,* and,
by recording that admission in the journals of
Parliament, to give them as strong an assurance
as the nature of the thing will admit, that we
mean for ever to adhere to that solemn declaration of systematic indulgence.

One fact is clear and indisputable. The public and avowed origin of this quarrel was on
taxation. This quarrel has, indeed, brought on
new disputes on new questions, but certainly
the least bitter, and the fewest of all, on the
trade laws. To judge which of the two be the
real radical cause of quarrel, we have to see
whether the commercial dispute did, in order
of time, precede the dispute on taxation. There
is not a shadow of evidence for it. Next, to
enable us to judge whether at this moment a
dislike to the trade laws be the real cause of
quarrel, it is absolutely necessary to put the
taxes out of the question by a repeal. See how
the Americans act in this position, and then
you will be able to discern correctly what is the
true object of the controversy, or whether any

controversy at all will remain. Unless you consent to remove this cause of difference, it is impossible, with decency, to assert that the dispute is not upon what it is avowed to be. And I would, sir, recommend to your serious consideration, whether it be prudent to form a rule for punishing people, not on their own acts, but on your conjectures. Surely it is preposterous at the very best. It is not justifying your anger by their misconduct, but it is converting your ill will into their delinquency.

You will now, sir, perhaps imagine that I am on the point of proposing to you a scheme for representation of the Colonies in Parliament. Perhaps I might be inclined to entertain some such thought, but a great flood stops me in my course. *Opposuit natura.* I can not remove the eternal barriers of the creation. The thing in that mode I do not know to be possible. As I meddle with no theory, I do not absolutely assert the impracticability of such a representation; but I do not see my way to it; and those who have been more confident have not been more successful. However, the arm of public benevolence is not shortened, and there are often several means to the same end. What nature has disjoined in one way wisdom may unite in another. When we can not give the benefit as we would wish, let us not refuse it altogether. If we can not give the principal, let us find a substitute. But how? Where? What substitute?

Fortunately I am not obliged for the ways and means of this substitute to tax my own unproductive invention. I am not even obliged to go to the rich treasury of the fertile framers of imaginary commonwealths; not to the Republic of Plato, not to the Utopia of More, not to the Oceana of Harrington. It is before me. It is at my feet.

> "And the dull swain
> Treads daily on it with his clouted shoon."

I only wish you to recognize, for the theory, the ancient constitutional policy of this kingdom with regard to representation, as that policy has been declared in acts of Parliament; and, as to the practise, to return to that mode which a uniform experience has marked out to you as best, and in which you walked with security, advantage, and honor, until the year 1763.[1]

My resolutions, therefore, mean to establish the equity and justice of a taxation of America, by *grant* and not by *imposition*. To mark the *legal competency* of the Colony assemblies for the support of their government in peace, and for public aids in time of war. To acknowledge that this legal competency has had *a dutiful and beneficial exercise;* and that experience has shown the *benefit of their grants,* and the

[1] That is, immediately after the Peace of Paris, when Great Britain sought to raise revenue in America by taxation without representation in order to defray some of the expense of the war in America with France.

futility of parliamentary taxation as a method of supply.

The conclusion is irresistible. You can not say that you were driven by any necessity to an exercise of the utmost rights of legislature. You can not assert that you took on yourselves the task of imposing Colony taxes, from the want of another legal body, that is competent to the purpose of supplying the exigencies of the State without wounding the prejudices of the people. Neither is it true that the body so qualified, and having that competence, had neglected the duty.

The question now on all this accumulated matter, is—whether you will choose to abide by a profitable experience, or a mischievous theory; whether you choose to build on imagination or fact; whether you prefer enjoyment or hope; satisfaction in your subjects or discontent.

The Americans will have no interest contrary to the grandeur and glory of England, when they are not oppressed by the weight of it; and they will rather be inclined to respect the acts of a superintending legislature, when they see them the acts of that power which is itself the security, not the rival, of their secondary importance. In this assurance my mind most perfectly acquiesces, and I confess I feel not the least alarm from the discontents which are to arise from putting people at their ease; nor do I apprehend the destruction of this Empire from giving, by an act of free grace and indulgence, to two millions of my fellow citizens, some share of those rights upon which I have always been taught to value myself.

It is said, indeed, that this power of granting, vested in American assemblies, would dissolve the unity of the Empire, which was preserved entire, altho Wales, and Chester, and Durham were added to it. Truly, Mr. Speaker, I do not know what this unity means, nor has it ever been heard of, that I know, in the constitutional policy of this country. The very idea of subordination of parts excludes this notion of simple and undivided unity. England is the head, but she is not the head and the members, too. Ireland has ever had from the beginning a separate, but not an independent legislature, which, far from distracting, promoted the union of the whole. Everything was sweetly and harmoniously disposed through both islands for the conservation of English dominion and the communication of English liberties. I do not see that the same principles might not be carried into twenty islands, and with the same good effect. This is my model with regard to America, as far as the internal circumstances of the two countries are the same. I know no other unity of this Empire than I can draw from its example during these periods, when it seemed to my poor understanding more united than it is now, or than it is likely to be by the present methods.

A revenue from America transmitted hither—do not delude yourselves—you never can receive it—no, not a shilling. We have experienced that from remote countries it is not to be expected. If, when you attempted to extract revenue from Bengal, you were obliged to return in loan what you had taken in imposition, what can you expect from North America? for certainly, if ever there was a country qualified to produce wealth, it is India; or an institution fit for the transmission, it is the East India Company. America has none of these aptitudes. If America gives you taxable objects on which you lay your duties *here*, and gives you, at the same time, a surplus by a foreign sale of her commodities to pay the duties on these objects which you tax at home, she has performed her part to the British revenue. But with regard to her own internal establishments, she may, I doubt not she will, contribute in moderation; I say in moderation, for she ought not to be permitted to exhaust herself. She ought to be reserved to a war, the weight of which, with the enemies that we are most likely to have, must be considerable in her quarter of the globe. There she may serve you, and serve you essentially.

For that service, for all service, whether of revenue, trade or empire, my trust is in her interest in the British Constitution. My hold of the Colonies is in the close affection which grows from common names, from kindred blood, from similar privileges, and equal protection. These are ties which, tho light as air, are as strong as links of iron. Let the Colonies always keep the idea of their civil rights associated with your government; they will cling and grapple to you, and no force under heaven will be of power to tear them from their allegiance. But let it be once understood that your government may be one thing, and their privileges another; that these two things may exist without any mutual relation; the cement is gone; the cohesion is loosened; and everything hastens to decay and dissolution.

As long as you have the wisdom to keep the sovereign authority of this country as the sanctuary of liberty, the sacred temple consecrated to our common faith; wherever the chosen race and sons of England worship Freedom, they will turn their faces toward you. The more they multiply, the more friends you will have. The more ardently they love liberty, the more perfect will be their obedience. Slavery they can have anywhere. It is a weed that grows in every soil. They may have it from Spain; they may have it from Prussia; but, until you become lost to all feeling of your true interest and your natural dignity, freedom they can have from none but you. This is the commodity of price, of which you have the monopoly. This is the true Act of Navigation, which binds to you the commerce of the Colonies, and through them secures to you the wealth of the world. Deny them this participation of freedom, and you break that sole bond which originally made, and must still preserve, the unity of the Empire. Do not entertain so weak an imagination as that your regis-

ters and your bonds, your affidavits and your
sufferances, your cockets and your clearances,
are what form the great securities of your commerce. Do not dream that your letters of office,
and your instructions, and your suspending
clauses, are the things that hold together the
great contexture of this mysterious whole.
These things do not make your government.
Dead instruments, passive tools as they are, it
is the spirit of the English communion that gives
all their life and efficacy to them. It is the
spirit of the English Constitution, which, in-
fused through the mighty mass, pervades, feeds,
unites, invigorates, vivifies every part of the
empire, even down to the minutest member.

All this, I know well enough, will sound wild
and chimerical to the profane herd of those
vulgar and mechanical politicians, who have no
place among us; a sort of people who think that
nothing exists but what is gross and material,
and who, therefore, far from being qualified to
be directors of the great movement of empire,
are not fit to turn a wheel in the machine. But
to men truly initiated and rightly taught, these
ruling and master principles, which, in the opinion of such men as I have mentioned, have no
substantial existence, are in truth everything
and all in all. Magnanimity in politics is not
seldom the truest wisdom; and a great empire and
little minds go ill together. If we are conscious
of our situation, and glow with zeal to fill our
place as becomes our station and ourselves, we

ought to auspicate all our public proceeding on America with the old warning of the Church, *sursum corda!* We ought to elevate our minds to the greatness of that trust to which the order of Providence has called us. By adverting to the dignity of this high calling, our ancestors have turned a savage wilderness into a glorious empire, and have made the most extensive and the only honorable conquests not by destroying, but by promoting, the wealth, the number, the happiness of the human race. Let us get an American revenue as we have got an American empire. English privileges have made it all that it is; English privileges alone will make it all that it can be.

II

PRINCIPLES IN POLITICS [1]
(1780)

THEY tell us that those of our fellow citizens whose chains we had a little relaxed are enemies to liberty and our free Constitution—not enemies, I presume, to their own liberty. And as to the Constitution, until we give them some share in it, I do not know on what pretense we can examine into their opinions about a business in which they have no interest or concern. But, after all, are we equally sure that they are ad-

[1] From his speech to the electors of Bristol in 1780.

verse to our Constitution as that our statutes are hostile and destructive to them? For my part, I have reason to believe their opinions and inclinations in that respect are various, exactly like those of other men. And if they lean more to the Crown than I, and that many of you think we ought, we must remember that he who aims at another's life is not to be surprised if he flies into any sanctuary that will receive him. The tenderness of the executive power is the natural asylum of those upon whom the laws have declared war; and to complain that men are inclined to favor the means of their own safety is so absurd that one forgets the injustice in the ridicule.

I must fairly tell you that, so far as my principles are concerned—principles that I hope will depart only with my last breath—I have no idea of a liberty unconnected with honesty and justice. Nor do I believe that any good constitutions of government or of freedom can find it necessary for their security to doom any part of the people to a permanent slavery. Such a constitution of freedom, if such can be, is in effect no more than another name for the tyranny of the strongest faction; and factions in republics have been, and are, fully as capable as monarchs, of the most cruel oppression and injustice. It is but too true that the love, and even the very idea, of genuine liberty is extremely rare. It is but too true that there are many whose whole scheme of freedom is made up of pride, perverseness, and insolence. They feel themselves in a state of thraldom; they imagine that their souls are cooped and cabined in, unless they have some man, or some body of men, dependent on their mercy. This desire of having some one below them descends to those who are the very lowest of all—and a Protestant cobbler, debased by his poverty, but exalted by his share of the ruling Church, feels a pride in knowing it is by his generosity alone, that the peer, whose footman's instep he measures, is able to keep his chaplain from a jail. This disposition is the true source of the passion which many men in very humble life have taken to the American war—our subjects in America, our Colonies, our dependents. This lust of party power is the liberty they hunger and thirst for; and this siren song of ambition has charmed ears that one would have thought were never organized to that sort of music.

This way of proscribing the citizens by denominations and general descriptions, dignified by the name of reasons of state, and security for constitutions and commonwealths, is nothing better at bottom than the miserable invention of an ungenerous ambition, which would fain hold the sacred trust of power, without any of the virtues or any of the energies that give a title to it; a receipt of policy, made up of a detestable compound of malice, cowardice, and sloth. They would govern men against their will, but in that government they would be discharged from the exercise of vigilance, providence, and fortitude; and, therefore, that they may sleep on their watch, they consent to take some one division of the society into partnership of the tyranny over the rest. But let government, in what form it may be, comprehend the whole in its justice, and restrain the suspicious by its vigilance; let it keep watch and ward; let it discover by its sagacity, and punish by its firmness, all delinquency against its power, whenever delinquency exists in the overt acts; and then it will be as safe as ever God and nature intended it should be. Crimes are the acts of individuals, and not of denominations, and therefore arbitrarily to class men under general descriptions, in order to proscribe and punish them in a lump for a presumed delinquency, of which perhaps but a part, perhaps none at all, are guilty, is indeed a compendious method, and saves a world of trouble about proof; but such a method, instead of being law, is an act of unnatural rebellion against the legal dominion of reason and justice, and this vice, in any constitution that entertains it, at one time or other, will certainly bring on its ruin.

We are told that this is not a religious persecution, and its abettors are loud in disclaiming all severities on account of conscience. Very fine, indeed! then let it be so! they are not persecutors; they are only tyrants. With all my heart! I am perfectly indifferent concerning the pretexts upon which we torment one another; or whether it be for the Constitution of the Church of England, or for the Constitution of the State of England, that people choose to make their fellow creatures wretched. When we were sent into a place of authority, you that sent us had yourselves but one commission to give. You could give us none to wrong or oppress, or even to suffer any kind of oppression or wrong, on any grounds whatsoever; not on political, as in the affairs of America; not on commercial, as in those of Ireland; not in civil, as in the laws for debt; not in religious, as in the statutes against Protestant or Catholic dissenters. The diversified but connected fabric of universal justice is well cramped and bolted together in all its parts; and depend upon it, I never have employed, and I never shall employ, any engine of power which may come into my hands, to wrench it asunder. All shall stand, if I can help it, and all shall stand connected. After all, to complete this work, much remains to be done; much in the East, much in the West. But great as the work is, if our will be ready, our powers are not deficient.

Since you have suffered me to trouble you so much on this subject, permit me, gentlemen, to detain you a little longer. I am, indeed, most solicitous to give you perfect satisfaction. I find there are some of a better and softer nature than the persons with whom I have supposed myself in debate, who neither think ill of the act of relief, nor by any means desire the repeal, not accusing but lamenting what was done, on account of the consequences, have frequently expressed their wish that the late act had never been made. Some of this description, and persons of worth, I have met with in this city. They conceive that the prejudices, whatever they might be, of a large part of the people, ought not to have been shocked; that their opinions ought to have been previously taken, and much attended to, and that thereby the late horrid scenes might have been prevented.

I confess my notions are widely different, and I never was less sorry for any action of my life. I like the Bill the better, on account of the events of all kinds that followed it. It relieved the real sufferers; it strengthened the State; and, by the disorders that ensued, we had clear evidence that there lurked a temper somewhere, which ought not to be fostered by the laws. No ill consequences whatever could be attributed to the Act itself. We knew beforehand, or we were poorly instructed, that toleration is odious to the intolerant, freedom to oppressors, property to robbers, and all kinds and degrees of prosperity to the envious. We knew that all these kinds of men would gladly gratify their evil dispositions under the sanction of law and religion, if they could; if they could not, yet, to make way to their objects, they would do their utmost to subvert all religion and all law. This we certainly knew. But knowing this, is there any reason,

because thieves break in and steal, and thus bring
detriment to you, and draw ruin on themselves,
that I am to be sorry that you are in possession
of shops, and of warehouses, and of wholesome
laws to protect them? Are you to build no
houses, because desperate men may pull them
down upon their own heads? Or, if a malignant
wretch will cut his own throat because he sees
you give alms to the necessitous and deserving,
shall his destruction be attributed to your charity, and not to his own deplorable madness? If
we repent of our good actions, what, I pray you,
is left for our faults and follies? It is not the
beneficence of the laws, it is the unnatural temper
which beneficence can fret and sour, that is to
be lamented. It is this temper which, by all
rational means, ought to be sweetened and corrected. If froward men should refuse this cure,
can they vitiate anything but themselves? Does
evil so react upon good, as not only to retard
its motion, but to change its nature? If it can
so operate, then good men will always be in the
power of the bad; and virtue, by a dreadful reverse of order, must lie under perpetual subjection and bondage of vice.

As to the opinion of the people, which some
think, in such cases, is to be implicitly obeyed,
nearly two years' tranquillity, which followed
the Act and its instant imitation in Ireland,
proved abundantly that the late horrible spirit
was, in a great measure, the effect of insidious
art and perverse industry and gross misrepre-

sentation. But, suppose that the dislike had been
much more deliberate and much more general
than I am persuaded it was. When we know
that the opinions of even the greatest multitudes
are the standard of rectitude, I shall think myself
obliged to make those opinions the masters of my
conscience. But if it may be doubted whether
omnipotence itself is competent to alter the es-
sential constitution of right and wrong, sure I
am that such things as they and I are possessed
of no such power. No man carries farther than
I do the policy of making government pleasing
to the people. But the widest range of this
politic complaisance is confined within the limits
of justice. I would not only consult the interests
of the people, but I would cheerfully gratify
their humors. We are all a sort of children that
must be soothed and managed. I think I am not
austere or formal in my nature. I would bear,
I would even myself play my part in, any innocent buffooneries to divert them. But I never
will act the tyrant for their amusement. If they
will mix malice in their sports I shall never consent to throw them any living, sentient creature
whatsoever; no, not so much as a kitling to torment.

"But if I profess all this impolitic stubborn-
ness, I may chance never to be elected into Parliament." It is certainly not pleasing to be put
out of the public service. But I wish to be a
member of Parliament to have my share of doing
good and resisting evil. It would, therefore, be

absurd to renounce my objects in order to obtain my seat. I deceive myself, indeed, most grossly, if I had not much rather pass the remainder of my life hidden in the recesses of the deepest obscurity, feeding my mind even with the visions and imaginations of such things, than to be placed on the most splendid throne of the universe, tantalized with a denial of the practise of all which can make the greatest situation any other than the greatest curse. Gentlemen, I have had my day. I can never sufficiently express my gratitude to you for having set me in a place wherein I could lend the slightest help to great and laudable designs. If I have had my share in any message giving quiet to private property and private conscience; if by my vote I have aided in securing to families the best possession, peace; if I have joined in reconciling kings to their subjects, and subjects to their prince; if I have assisted to loosen the foreign holdings of the citizen, and taught him to look for his protection to the laws of the country, and for his comfort to the good will of his countrymen; if I have thus taken my part with the best of men in the best of their actions, I can shut the book. I might wish to read a page or two more, but this is enough for my measure—I have not lived in vain.

And now, gentlemen, on this serious day, when I come, as it were, to make up my account with you, let me take to myself some degree of honest pride on the nature of the charges that are against me. I do not stand here before you accused of venality, or of neglect of duty. It is not said, that, in the long period of my service, I have, in a single instance, sacrificed the slightest of your interests to my ambition or to my fortune. It is not alleged that to gratify any anger or revenge of my own, or of my party, I have had a share in wronging or oppressing any description of men or any one man in any description. No! the charges against me are all of one kind: that I have pushed the principles of general justice and benevolence too far; farther than a cautious policy would warrant, and farther than the opinions of many would go along with me. In every accident which may happen through life, in pain, in sorrow, in depression, and in distress, I will call to mind this accusation, and be comforted.

III

AT THE TRIAL OF WARREN HASTINGS [1]
(1788)

My LORDS, you have now heard the principles
on which Mr. Hastings governs the part of Asia
subjected to the British Empire. Here he has
declared his opinion that he is a despotic prince;
that he is to use arbitrary power; and, of course,
all his acts are covered with that shield. "I
know," says he, "the Constitution of Asia only
from its practise." Will your lordships submit
to hear the corrupt practises of mankind made
the principles of government? *He* have arbitrary power!—my lords, the East India Company have not arbitrary power to give him; the
king has no arbitrary power to give him; your

---

[1] From his speech before the High Court of Impeachment, in
Westminster Hall, February, 1788. It was of this speech that Hastings said, "For the first half hour, I looked up to the orator in a
reverie of wonder, and during that time I felt myself the most
culpable man on earth." Burke spoke during four sittings, beginning on February 13. Macaulay in his essay on Warren
Hastings, has described this memorable scene:

"There have been spectacles more dazzling to the eye, more
gorgeous with jewelry and cloth of gold, more attractive to grown-
up children, than that which was then exhibited at Westminster,
but perhaps, there was never a spectacle so well calculated to
strike a highly cultivated, a reflecting, an imaginative mind. All
the various kinds of interest which belong to the near and to the
distant, to the present, and to the past, were collected on one spot,
and in one hour. All the talents and all the accomplishments

lordships have not; nor the Commons; nor the whole Legislature.

We have no arbitrary power to give, because arbitrary power is a thing which neither any man can hold nor any man can give. No man can lawfully govern himself according to his own will—much less can one person be governed by the will of another. We are all born in subjection—all born equally, high and low, governors and governed, in subjection to one great, immutable, preexistent law, prior to all our devices, and prior to all our contrivances, paramount to all our ideas and to all our sensations, antecedent to our very existence, by which we are knit and connected in the eternal frame of the universe, out of which we can not stir.

This great law does not arise from our conventions or compacts; on the contrary, it gives to our conventions and compacts all the force and

which are developed by liberty and civilization were now displayed; with every advantage that could be derived both from cooperation and from contrast.

"Every step in the proceedings carried the mind either backward, through many troubled centuries, to the days when the foundations of our Constitution were laid; or far away, over boundless seas and deserts, to dusky nations living under strange stars, worshiping strange gods, and writing strange characters from right to left. The High Court of Parliament was to sit, according to forms handed down from the days of the Plantagenets, on an Englishman accused of exercising tyranny over the lord of the holy city of Benares, and over the ladies of the princely house of Oude.

"The place was worthy of such a trial. It was the great hall of

sanction they can have: it does not arise from
our vain institutions. Every good gift is of
God, all power is of God; and He who has
given the power, and from whom alone it
originates, will never suffer the exercise of it
to be practised upon any less solid foundation
than the power itself.

If, then, all dominion of man over man is the
effect of the divine disposition, it is bound by the
eternal laws of Him that gave it, with which
no human authority can dispense; neither he
that exercises it, nor even those who are subject
to it; and, if they were mad enough to make
an express compact, that should release their
magistrate from his duty, and should declare
their lives, liberties and properties, dependent
upon, not rules and laws, but his mere capri-
cious will, that covenant would be void.

This arbitrary power is not to be had by conquest. Nor can any sovereign have it by suc-

William Rufus; the hall which had resounded with acclamations at
the inauguration of thirty kings; the hall which had witnessed the
just sentence of Bacon and the just absolution of Somers; the hall
where the eloquence of Strafford had for a moment awed and
melted a victorious party inflamed with just resentment; the hall
where Charles had confronted the High Court of Justice with the
placid courage which has half redeemed his fame.

"Neither military nor civil pomp was wanting. The avenues
were lined with grenadiers. The streets were kept clear by cavalry.
The peers, robed in gold and ermine, were marshaled by the heralds
under Garter king-at-arms. The judges in their vestments of
state attended to give advice on points of law. Near a hundred
and seventy lords, three-fourths as the Upper House then was,
walked in solemn order from their usual place of assembling to the

cession; for no man can succeed to fraud, rapine, and violence. Those who give and those who receive arbitrary power are alike criminal; and there is no man but is bound to resist it to the best of his power, wherever it shall show its face to the world.

Law and arbitrary power are in eternal enmity. Name me a magistrate, and I will name property; name me power, and I will name protection. It is a contradiction in terms, it is blasphemy in religion, it is wickedness in politics, to say that any man can have arbitrary power. In every patent of office the duty is included. For what else does a magistrate exist? To suppose for power, is an absurdity in idea. Judges are guided and governed by the eternal laws of justice, to which we are all subject. We may bite our chains, if we will; but we shall be made to know ourselves, and be taught that man is born to be governed by *law;* and he that will

tribunal. The junior baron present led the way, George Eliott, Lord Heathfield, recently ennobled for his memorable defense of Gibraltar against the fleets and armies of France and Spain. The long procession was closed by the Duke of Norfolk, earl marshal of the realm, by the great dignitaries, and by the brothers and the sons of the king. Last of all came the Prince of Wales, conspicuous by his fine person and noble bearing.

"The grey old walls were hung with scarlet. The long galleries were crowded by an audience such as has rarely excited the fears or the emulation of an orator. There were gathered together, from all parts of a great, free, enlightened, and prosperous Empire, grace and female loveliness, wit and learning, the representatives of every science and of every art. There were seated around the queen the fair-haired young daughters of the house of Brunswick.

substitute *will* in the place of it is an enemy to God.

My lords, I do not mean now to go farther than just to remind your lordships of this—that Mr. Hastings' government was one whole system of oppression, of robbery of individuals, of spoliation of the public, and of supersession of the whole system of the English government, in order to vest in the worst of the natives all the power that could possibly exist in any government; in order to defeat the ends which all governments ought, in common, to have in view. In the name of the Commons of England, I charge all this villainy upon Warren Hastings, in this last moment of my application to you.

My lords, what is it that we want here, to a great act of national justice? Do we want a cause, my lords? You have the cause of oppressed princes, of undone women of the first rank, of desolated provinces, and of wasted kingdoms.

There the ambassadors of great kings and commonwealths gazed with admiration on a spectacle which no other country in the world could present. There Siddons, in the prime of her majestic beauty, looked with emotion on a scene surpassing all the imitations of the stage. There the historian of the Roman Empire thought of the days when Cicero pleaded the cause of Sicily against Verres, and when, before a senate which still retained some show of freedom, Tacitus thundered against the oppressor of Africa.

"There were seen, side by side, the greatest painter and the greatest scholar of the age. The spectacle had allured Reynolds from that easel which has preserved to us the thoughtful foreheads of so many writers and statesmen, and the sweet smiles of so many noble matrons. It had induced Parr to suspend his labors in that

Do you want a criminal, my lords? When was there so much iniquity ever laid to the charge of any one? No, my lords, you must not look to punish any other such delinquent from India. Warren Hastings has not left substance enough in India to nourish such another delinquent.

My lords, is it a prosecutor you want? You have before you the Commons of Great Britain as prosecutors; and I believe, my lords, that the sun, in his beneficent progress round the world, does not behold a more glorious sight than that of men, separated from a remote people by the material bounds and barriers of nature, united by the bond of a social and moral community—all the Commons of England resenting, as their own, the indignities and cruelties that are offered to all the people of India.

Do we want a tribunal? My lords, no example of antiquity, nothing in the modern world,

dark and profound mine from which he had extracted a vast treasure of erudition—a treasure too often buried in the earth, too often paraded with injudicious and inelegant ostentation, but still precious, massive, and splendid. There appeared the voluptuous charms of her to whom the heir of the throne had in secret plighted his faith. There, too, was she, the beautiful mother of a beautiful race, the Saint Cecilia, whose delicate features, lighted up by love and music, art has rescued from the common decay. There were the members of that brilliant society which quoted, criticized, and exchanged repartees, under the rich peacock-hangings of Mrs. Montague. And there the ladies whose lips, more persuasive than those of Fox himself, had carried the Westminster election against palace and treasury, shone round Georgiana, Duchess of Devonshire."

nothing in the range of human imagination, can supply us with a tribunal like this. We commit safely the interests of India and humanity into your hands. Therefore, it is with confidence that, ordered by the Commons,

I impeach Warren Hastings, Esquire, of high crimes and misdemeanors.

I impeach him in the name of the Commons of Great Britain in Parliament assembled, whose parliamentary trust he has betrayed.

I impeach him in the name of all the Commons of Great Britain, whose national character he has dishonored.

I impeach him in the name of the people of India, whose laws, rights and liberties he has subverted; whose properties he has destroyed; whose country he has laid waste and desolate.

I impeach him in the name and by virtue of those eternal laws of justice which he has violated.

I impeach him in the name of human nature itself, which he has cruelly outraged, injured and oppressed, in both sexes, in every age, rank, situation, and condition of life.

My lords, at this awful close, in the name of the Commons and surrounded by them, I attest the retiring, I attest the advancing generations, between which, as a link in the great chain of eternal order, we stand. We call this nation, we call the world to witness, that the Commons have shrunk from no labor; that we have been guilty of no prevarication; that we have made no compromise with crime; that we have not feared any odium whatsoever, in the long warfare which we have carried on with the crimes, with the vices, with the exorbitant wealth, with the enormous and overpowering influence of Eastern corruption.

My lords, it has pleased Providence to place us in such a state that we appear every moment to be upon the verge of some great mutations. There is one thing, and one thing only, which defies all mutation: that which existed before the world, and will survive the fabric of the world itself—I mean justice; that justice which, emanating from the Divinity, has a place in the breast of every one of us, given us for our guide with regard to ourselves and with regard to others, and which will stand, after this globe is burned to ashes, our advocate or our accuser, before the great Judge, when He comes to call upon us for the tenor of a well-spent life.

My lords, the Commons will share in every fate with your lordships; there is nothing sinister which can happen to you, in which we shall not all be involved; and, if it should so happen that we shall be subjected to some of those frightful changes which we have seen— if it should happen that your lordships, stripped of all the decorous distinctions of human society, should, by hands at once base and cruel, be led to those scaffolds and machines of murder upon which great kings and glorious queens have shed their blood, amidst the prelates, amidst the nobles, amidst the magistrates, who supported their thrones—may you in those moments feel that consolation which I am persuaded they felt in the critical moments of their dreadful agony!

My lords, if you must fall, may you so fall! but, if you stand—and stand I trust you will—together with the fortune of this ancient monarchy, together with the ancient laws and liberties of this great and illustrious kingdom, may you stand as unimpeached in honor as in power; may you stand, not as a substitute for virtue, but as an ornament of virtue, as a security for virtue; may you stand long, and long stand the terror of tyrants; may you stand the refuge of afflicted nations; may you stand a sacred temple, for the perpetual residence of an inviolable justice!

GRATTAN

I

A PLEA FOR IRISH LEGISLATIVE INDEPENDENCE[1]

(1780)

Born in 1746, died in 1820; was admitted to the Irish Bar in 1772, entered the Irish Parliament in 1775; secured the restoration of independence to the Irish Parliament in 1782; retired from the Irish Parliament in 1797; returned to the Irish Parliament in 1800, in order to oppose the Union; elected to the Imperial Parliament in 1806, remaining a member until his death.

SIR, I have entreated an attendance on this day that you might, in the most public manner, deny the claim of the British Parliament to make law for Ireland, and with one voice lift up your hands against it.

If I had lived when the 9th of William took away the woolen manufacture, or when the 6th of George I. declared this country to be dependent and subject to laws to be enacted by the Parliament of England, I should have made a covenant with my own conscience to seize the first moment of rescuing my country from the ignominy of such acts of power; or, if I had a son, I should have administered to him an oath that he would consider himself a person separate

[1] From a speech delivered in the Irish Parliament, April 19, 1780, and described by Hardy in his "Life of Lord Charlemontt" as "never to be forgotten by those who heard it." In May, 1782, the Imperial Parliament passed the act declaring the Irish Parliament independent.

and set apart for the discharge of so important a duty; upon the same principle I am now come to move a Declaration of Right, the first moment occurring, since my time, in which such a declaration could be made with any chance of success, and without aggravation of oppression.

Sir, it must appear to every person that, notwithstanding the import of sugar and export of woolens, the people of this country are not satisfied—something remains; the greater work is behind; the public heart is not well at ease. To promulgate our satisfactions; to stop the throats of millions with the votes of Parliament; to preach homilies to the volunteers; to utter invectives against the people, under pretense of affectionate advice, is an attempt, weak, suspicious and inflammatory.

You can not dictate to those whose sense you are intrusted to represent; your ancestors, who sat within these walls, lost to Ireland trade and liberty; you, by the assistance of the people, have recovered trade; you still owe the kingdom liberty; she calls upon you to restore it.

The ground of public discontent seems to be: "We have gotten commerce, but no freedom"; the same power which took away the export of woolens and the export of glass may take them away again; the repeal is partial, and the ground of repeal is upon a principle of expediency.

Sir, "expedient" is a word of appropriated and tyrannical import; "expedient" is an ill-omened word, selected to express the reservation of authority, while the exercise is mitigated; "expedient" is the ill-omened expression of the Repeal of the American Stamp Act. England thought it "expedient" to repeal that law; happy had it been for mankind, if, when she withdrew the exercise, she had not reserved the right![1] To that reservation she owes the loss of her American empire, at the expense of millions, and America the seeking of liberty through a sea of bloodshed. The repeal of the Woolen Act, similarly circumstanced, pointed against the principle of our liberty—a present relaxation, but tyranny in reserve—may be a subject for illumination to a populace, or a pretense for apostasy to a courtier, but can not be the subject of settled satisfaction to a freeborn, intelligent, and injured community.

Nor are we only prompted to this when we consider our strength; we are challenged to it when we look to Great Britain. The people of that country are now waiting to hear the Parliament of Ireland speak on the subject of their liberty; it begins to be made a question in England whether the principal persons wish to be free; it was the delicacy of former Parliaments to be silent on the subject of commercial restrictions, lest they should show a knowledge of the fact, and not a sense of the violation; you have spoken out, you have shown a knowledge of the

[1] The tea tax, a source of small revenue, was imposed merely that England might keep the right to tax the Colonies. The Boston Tea Party was a means resorted to for denying that right.

fact, and not a sense of the violation. On the contrary, you have returned thanks for a partial repeal made on a principle of power; you have returned thanks as for a favor, and your exultation has brought your characters, as well as your spirit, into question, and tends to shake to her foundation your title to liberty; thus you do not leave your rights where you found them. You have done too much not to do more; you have gone too far not to go on; you have brought yourselves into that situation in which you must silently abdicate the rights of your country, or publicly restore them. It is very true you may feed your manufacturers, and landed gentlemen may get their rents, and you may export woolen, and may load a vessel with baize, serges, and kerseys, and you may bring back again directly from the plantations sugar, indigo, speckle-wood, beetle-root, and panellas. But liberty, the foundation of trade, the charters of the land, the independency of Parliament, the securing, crowning, and the consummation of everything are yet to come. Without them the work is imperfect, the foundation is wanting, the capital is wanting, trade is not free, Ireland is a colony without the benefit of a charter, and you are a provincial synod without the privileges of a Parliament.

The British minister mistakes the Irish character: had he intended to make Ireland a slave, he should have kept her a beggar; there is no middle policy; win her heart by the restoration of her right, or cut off the nation's right hand; greatly emancipate, or fundamentally destroy it. We may talk plausibly to England, but so long as she exercises a power to bind this country, so long are the nations in a state of war; the claims of the one go against the liberty of the other, and the sentiments of the latter go to oppose these claims to the last drop of her blood. The English Opposition, therefore, are right; mere trade will not satisfy Ireland—they judge of us by other great nations, by the nation whose political life has been a struggle for liberty; they judge of us with a true knowledge of, and just deference for, our character—that a country enlightened as Ireland, chartered as Ireland, armed as Ireland, and injured as Ireland, will be satisfied with nothing less than liberty.

There is no objection to this resolution, except fears; I have examined your fears; I pronounce them to be frivolous. I might deny that the British nation was attached to the idea of binding Ireland; I might deny that England was a tyrant at heart; and I might call to witness the odium of North and the popularity of Chatham, her support of Holland, her contributions to Corsica, and her charters communicated to Ireland; but ministers have traduced England to debase Ireland; and politicians, like priests, represent the power they serve as diabolical, to possess with superstitious fears the victim whom they design to plunder. If England is a tyrant, it is you who have made her so; it is the slave that makes the tyrant, and then murmurs at the master whom he himself has constituted.

I do allow, on the subject of commerce, England was jealous in the extreme, and I do say it was commercial jealousy, it was the spirit of monopoly (the woolen trade and the Act of Navigation had made her tenacious of a comprehensive legislative authority), and having now ceded that monopoly, there is nothing in the way of your liberty except your own corruption and pusillanimity; and nothing can prevent your being free except yourselves. It is not in the disposition of England; it is not in the interest of England; it is not in her arms. What! can 8,000,000 of Englishmen opposed to 20,000,000 of French, to 7,000,000 of Spanish, to 3,000,000 of Americans, reject the alliance of 3,000,000 in Ireland? Can 8,000,000 of British men, thus outnumbered by foes, take upon their shoulders the expense of an expedition to enslave you? Will Great Britain, a wise and magnanimous country, thus tutored by experience and wasted by war, the French Navy riding her Channel, send an army to Ireland, to levy no tax, to enforce no law, to answer no end whatsoever, except to spoliate the charters of Ireland and enforce a barren oppression? What? has England lost thirteen Provinces? has she reconciled herself to this loss, and will she not be reconciled to the liberty of Ireland? Take notice that the very constitution which I move you to declare

Great Britain herself offered to America; it is a very instructive proceeding in the British history. In 1778 a commission went out, with powers to cede to the thirteen Provinces of America, totally and radically, the legislative authority claimed over her by the British Parliament, and the commissioners, pursuant to their powers, did offer to all or any of the American States the total surrender of the legislative authority of the British Parliament.[1]

What! has England offered this to the resistance of America, and will she refuse it to the loyalty of Ireland? Your fears, then, are nothing but a habitual subjugation of mind; that subjugation of mind which made you, at first, tremble at every great measure of safety; which made the principal men among us conceive the commercial association would be a war; that fear, which made them imagine the military association had a tendency to treason; which made them think a short money bill would be a public convulsion; and yet these measures have not only proved to be useful, but are held to be moderate, and the Parliament that adopted them, is praised, not for its unanimity only, but for its temper also. You now wonder that you submitted for so many years to the loss of the woolen trade and the deprivation of the glass trade; raised above your former abject state in commerce, you were ashamed at your past

[1] The British commissioners came to America with an offer to repeal the tea tax and to renounce the right to raise revenue.

pusillanimity; so when you have summoned a boldness which shall assert the liberties of your country—raised by the act, and reinvested, as you should be, in the glory of your ancient rights and privileges, you will be surprised at yourselves, who have so long submitted to their violation. Moderation is but the relative term; for nations, like men, are only safe in proportion to the spirit they put forth, and the proud contemplation with which they survey themselves. Conceive yourselves a plantation, ridden by an oppressive government, and everything you have done is but a fortunate frenzy; conceive yourselves to be what you are, a great, a growing, and a proud nation, and a declaration of right is no more than the safe exercise of your indubitable authority.

I shall hear of ingratitude! I name the argument to despise it and the men who make use of it; I know the men who use it are not grateful, they are insatiate; they are public extortioners, who would stop the tide of public prosperity and turn it to the channel of their own emolument; I know of no species of gratitude which should prevent my country from being free, no gratitude which should oblige Ireland to be the slave of England. In cases of robbery and usurpation, nothing is an object of gratitude except the thing stolen, the charter spoliated. A nation's liberty can not, like her treasures, be meted and parceled out in gratitude; no man can be grateful or liberal of his conscience, nor woman of her honor, nor nation of her liberty; there are certain unimpartable, inherent, invaluable properties, not to be alienated from the person, whether body politic or body natural. With the same contempt do I treat that charge which says that Ireland is insatiable; saying that Ireland asks nothing but that which Great Britain has robbed her of, her rights and privileges; to say that Ireland will not be satisfied with liberty, because she is not satisfied with slavery, is folly. I laugh at that man who supposes that Ireland will not be content with a free trade and a free constitution; and would any man advise her to be content with less?

The same laws, the same charters, communicate to both kingdoms, Great Britain and Ireland, the same rights and privileges; and one privilege above them all is that communicated by Magna Charta, by the 25th of Edward III., and by a multitude of other statutes, "not to be bound by any act except made with the archbishops, bishops, earls, barons, and freemen of the commonalty," namely, of the Parliament of the realm. On this right of exclusive legislation are founded the Petition of Right, Bill of Rights, Revolution, and Act of Settlement. The king has no other title to his crown than that which you have to your liberty; both are founded, the throne and your freedom, upon the right vested in the subject to resist by arms, notwithstanding the oaths of allegiance, any authority attempting to impose acts of power as laws, whether that authority be one man or a host, the second James, or the British Parliament!

Every argument for the House of Hanover is equally an argument for the liberties of Ireland; the Act of Settlement is an act of rebellion, or the declaratory statute of the 6th of George I., an act of usurpation; for both can not be law.

I do not refer to doubtful history, but to living record; to common charters; to the interpretation England has put upon these charters—an interpretation not made by words only, but crowned by arms; to the revolution she had formed upon them, to the king she has deposed, and to the king she has established; and, above all, to the oath of allegiance solemnly plighted to the House of Stuart, and afterward set aside, in the instance of a grave and moral people absolved by virtue of these very charters.

And as anything less than liberty is inadequate to Ireland, so is it dangerous to Great Britain. We are too near the British nation, we are too conversant with her history, we are too much fired by her example, to be anything less than her equal; anything less, we should be her bitterest enemies—an enemy to that power which smote us with her mace, and to that Constitution from whose blessings we were excluded: to be ground as we have been by the British nation, bound by her Parliament, plundered by her Crown, threatened by her enemies, insulted with her protection, while we return thanks for her condescension, or a system of meanness and misery which has expired in our determination, as I hope it has in her magnanimity.

There is no policy left for Great Britain but to cherish the remains of her Empire, and do justice to a country who is determined to do justice to herself, certain that she gives nothing equal to what she received from us when we gave her Ireland.

Do not tolerate that power which blasted you for a century, that power which shattered your loom, banished your manufacturers, dishonored your peerage, and stopped the growth of your people; do not, I say, be bribed by an export of woolen, or an import of sugar, and permit that power which has thus withered the land to remain in your country and have existence in your pusillanimity.

Do not suffer the arrogance of England to imagine a surviving hope in the fears of Ireland; do not send the people to their own resolves for liberty, passing by the tribunals of justice and the high court of Parliament; neither imagine that, by any formation of apology, you can palliate such a commission to your hearts, still less to your children, who will sting you with their curses in your grave for having interposed between them and their Maker, robbing them of an immense occasion, and losing an opportunity which you did not create, and can never restore.

Hereafter, when these things shall be history,

your age of thraldom and poverty, your sudden resurrection, commercial redress, and miraculous armament, shall the historian stop at liberty, and observe that here the principal men among us fell into mimic trances of gratitude— they were awed by a weak ministry, and bribed by an empty treasury—and when liberty was within their grasp, and the temple opened her folding-doors, and the arms of the people clanged, and the zeal of the nation urged and encouraged them on, that they fell down and were prostituted at the threshold?

I might, as a constituent, come to your bar, and demand my liberty. I do call upon you, by the laws of the land and their violation, by the instruction of eighteen counties, by the arms, inspiration, and providence of the present moment, tell us the rule by which we shall go— assert the law of Ireland—declare the liberty of the land.

I will not be answered by a public lie, in the shape of an amendment; neither, speaking for the subject's freedom, am I to hear of faction. I wish for nothing but to breathe, in this our island, in common with my fellow subjects, the air of liberty. I have no ambition, unless it be the ambition to break your chain and contemplate your glory. I never will be satisfied so long as the meanest cottager in Ireland has a link of the British chain clanking to his rags— he may be naked, he shall not be in iron; and I do see the time is at hand, the spirit is gone forth, the declaration is planted; and tho great men shall apostatize, yet the cause will live; and tho the public speaker should die, yet the immortal fire shall outlast the organ which conveyed it, and the breath of liberty, like the word of the holy man, will not die with the prophet, but survive him.

II

INVECTIVE AGAINST CORRY [1]

(1800)

HAS the gentleman done? Has he completely done? He was unparliamentary from the beginning to the end of his speech. There was scarce a word he uttered that was not a violation of the privileges of the House; but I did not call him to order—why? because the limited talents of some men render it impossible for them to be severe without being unparliamentary. But before I sit down I shall show him how to be severe and parliamentary at the same time. On any other occasion I should think myself justifiable in treating with silent contempt anything which might fall from that honorable member; but there are times when the insignificance of the accuser is lost in the magnitude of the accusation. I know the difficulty the honorable gentleman labored under

[1] From a speech delivered in the Irish Parliament, February 14, 1800.

when he attacked me, conscious that, on a comparative view of our characters, public and private, there is nothing he could say which would injure me. The public would not believe the charge. I despise the falsehood. If such a charge were made by an honest man, I would answer it in the manner I shall do before I sit down. But I shall first reply to it when not made by an honest man.

The right honorable gentleman has called me "an unimpeached traitor." I ask, why not "traitor," unqualified by any epithet? I will tell him: it was because he dare not. It was the act of a coward, who raises his arm to strike, but has not courage to give the blow. I will not call him villain, because it would be unparliamentary, and he is a privy counselor. I will not call him fool, because he happens to be chancellor of the exchequer. But I say he is one who has abused the privilege of Parliament and freedom of debate to the uttering language, which, if spoken out of the House, I should answer only with a blow. I care not how high his situation, how low his character, how contemptible his speech; whether a privy counselor or a parasite, my answer would be a blow. He has charged me with being connected with the rebels: the charge is utterly, totally, and meanly false. Does the honorable gentleman rely on the report of the House of Lords for the foundation of his assertion? If he does, I can prove to the committee there was a physical impossibility of that report being true. But I scorn to answer any man for my conduct, whether he be a political coxcomb, or whether he brought himself into power by a false glare of courage or not. I scorn to answer any wizard of the Castle throwing himself into fantastical airs. But if an honorable and independent man were to make a charge against me, I would say: "You charge me with having an intercourse with the rebels, and you found your charge upon what is said to have appeared before a committee of the lords. Sir, the report of that committee is totally and egregiously irregular." I will read a letter from Mr. Nelson, who had been examined before that committee; it states that what the report represents him as having spoken is not what he said.

From the situation that I held, and from the connections I had in the City of Dublin, it was necessary for me to hold intercourse with various descriptions of persons. The right honorable member might as well have been charged with a participation in the guilt of those traitors; for he had communicated with some of those very persons on the subject of parliamentary reform. The Irish government, too, were in communication with some of them.

The right honorable member has told me I deserted a profession where wealth and station were the reward of industry and talent. If I mistake not, that gentleman endeavored to obtain those rewards by the same means; but he soon deserted the occupation of a barrister for those of a parasite and pander. He fled from the labor of study to flatter at the table of the great. He found the lords' parlor a better sphere for his exertions than the hall of the Four Courts; the house of a great man a more convenient way to power and place; and that it was easier for a statesman of middling talents to sell his friends, than for a lawyer of no talents to sell his clients.

For myself, whatever corporate or other bodies have said or done to me, I from the bottom of my heart forgive them. I feel I have done too much for my country to be vexed at them. I would rather that they should not feel or acknowledge what I have done for them, and call me traitor, than have reason to say I sold them. I will always defend myself against the assassin; but with large bodies it is different. To the people I will bow: they may be my enemy—I never shall be theirs.

At the emancipation of Ireland, in 1782, I took a leading part in the foundation of that Constitution which is now endeavored to be destroyed. Of that Constitution I was the author; in that Constitution I glory; and for it the honorable gentleman should bestow praise, not invent calumny. Notwithstanding my weak state of body, I come to give my last testimony against this union, so fatal to the liberties and interests of my country. I come to make common cause with these honorable and virtuous gentlemen around me; to try to save the Constitution; or if not to save the Constitution, at least to save our characters, and remove from our graves the foul disgrace of standing apart while a deadly blow is aimed at the independence of our country.

The right honorable gentleman says I fled from the country after exciting rebellion, and that I have returned to raise another. No such thing. The charge is false. The civil war had not commenced when I left the kingdom; and I could not have returned without taking a part. On one side there was the camp of the rebel; on the other, the camp of the minister, a greater traitor than that rebel. The stronghold of the Constitution was nowhere to be found. I agree that the rebel who rose against the government should have suffered; but I missed on the scaffold the right honorable gentleman. Two desperate parties were in arms against the Constitution. The right honorable gentleman belonged to one of those parties and deserved death. I could not join the rebel; I could not join the government; I could not join torture; I could not join half-hanging; I could not join free quarter; I could take part with neither. I was therefore absent from a scene where I could not be active without self-reproach, nor indifferent with safety.

Many honorable gentlemen thought differently from me; I respect their opinions, but I keep my own; and I think now, as I thought then, that the treason of the minister against the liberties of the people was infinitely worse than the rebellion of the people against the minister.

I have returned, not as the right honorable member has said, to raise another storm; I have returned to discharge an honorable debt of gratitude to my country, that conferred a great reward for past services, which, I am proud to say, was not greater than my desert. I have returned to protect that Constitution, of which I was the parent and founder, from the assassination of such men as the honorable gentleman and his unworthy associates. They are corrupt; they are seditious; and they, at this very moment, are in a conspiracy against their country. I have returned to refute a libel as false as it is malicious, given to the public under the appellation of a report of a committee of the lords. Here I stand ready for impeachment or trial; I dare accusation. I defy the honorable gentleman; I defy the government; I defy their whole phalanx; let them come forth. I tell the ministers I will neither give them quarter nor take it. I am here to lay the shattered remains of my Constitution on the floor of this House in defense of the liberties of my country.

SHERIDAN

AT THE TRIAL OF WARREN HASTINGS [1]
(1788)

Born in 1751, died in 1816; settled in London in 1773; Proprietor
of Drury Lane Theater in 1776; entered Parliament in 1780; Secretary of the Treasury in 1783; Treasurer of the Navy in 1806; left
Parliament in 1812; author of "The School for Scandal," 1777.

IF a stranger had at this time [in 1782] gone
into the kingdom of Oude, ignorant of what had
happened since the death of Sujah Dowlah—that
man who with a savage heart had still great lines
of character, and who with all his ferocity in
war, had still with a cultivating hand preserved
to his country the riches which it derived from
benignant skies, and a prolific soil—if this
stranger, ignorant of all that had happened in
the short interval, and observing the wide and
general devastation, and all the horrors of the
scene—of plains unclothed and brown—of vege-
tation burnt up and extinguished—of villages

---

[1] From Sheridan's speech as delivered before Parliament sitting
as a High Court in Westminster Hall, on June 3, 6, 10 and 13, in
1788, when as much as fifty pounds was known to be paid for a
seat. When Sheridan had spoken the final word, "My lords, I
have done," he was caught by Burke in his arms and "hugged
with the energy of generous admiration." So says Macaulay, but
Macaulay represents that Sheridan "contrived with a knowledge
of stage effect which his father might have envied, to sink back, as
if exhausted, into the arms of Burke." Only one of Sheridan's
speeches has been preserved in anything approaching an adequate
report.

depopulated and in ruin—of temples unroofed and perishing—of reservoirs broken down and dry—he would naturally inquire, What war had thus laid waste the fertile fields of this once beautiful and opulent country? What civil dissensions have happened thus to tear asunder, and separate the happy societies that once possessed those villages? What religious rage had, with unholy violence, demolished those temples, and disturbed fervent, but unobtruding piety in the exercise of its duties? What merciless enemy had thus spread the horrors of fire and sword? What severe visitation of Providence had thus dried up the mountains, and taken from the face of the earth every vestige of green?—or rather, what monsters had crawled over the country, tainting and poisoning what the voracious appetite could not devour? To such questions, what must be the answer? No wars have ravaged these lands and depopulated these villages—no civil discords have been felt—no religious rage—no merciless enemy—no affliction of Providence which, while it scourged for the moment, cut off the sources of resuscitation—no voracious and poisoning monsters—no; all this has been accomplished by the friendship, generosity, and kindness of the English nation. They had embraced us with their protecting arms—and, lo, these are the fruits of their alliance.

There is nothing, my lords, to be found in the history of human turpitude; nothing in the nervous delineations and penetrating brevity of

Tacitus; nothing in the luminous and luxuriant pages of Gibbon,[1] or of any other historian, dead or living, who, searching into measures and characters with the rigor of truth, presents to our abhorrence depravity in its blackest shapes, which can equal, in the grossness of the guilt, or in the hardness of heart with which it was conducted, or in low and groveling motives, the acts and character of the prisoner. It was he who, in the base desire of stripping two helpless women, could stir the son to rise up in vengeance against them; who, when that son had certain touches of nature in his breast, certain feelings of an awakened conscience, could accuse him of entertaining peevish objections to the plunder and sacrifice of his mother; who, having finally divested him of all thought, all reflection, all memory, all conscience, all tenderness and duty as a son, all dignity as a monarch; having destroyed his character, and depopulated his country, at length brought him to violate the dearest ties of nature, in countenancing the destruction of his parents.

This crime, I say, has no parallel or prototype in the Old World or the New, from the day of original sin to the present hour. The victims of his oppression were confessedly destitute of all power to resist their oppressors. But their

---

[1] This graceful tribute to Gibbon who was present to hear it, has suffered somewhat from a fiction that represents Sheridan as saying afterward that he meant " voluminous " instead of " luminous." Moore, Sheridan's biographer, is said to be responsible for the fiction.

debility, which from other bosoms would have claimed some compassion, at least with respect to the mode of suffering, with him excited only the ingenuity of torture. Even when every feeling of the Nabob was subdued; when, as we have seen, my lords, nature made a last, lingering, feeble stand within his breast; even then, that cold, unfriendly spirit of malignity, with which his doom was fixed, returned with double rigor and sharper acrimony to its purpose, and compelled the child to inflict on the parent that destruction of which he was himself reserved to be the final victim.

Great as is this climax in which, my lords, I thought the pinnacle of guilt was attained, there is yet something still more transcendently flagitious. I particularly allude to his infamous letter, falsely dated the 15th of February, 1782, in which, at the very moment that he had given the order for the entire destruction of the Begums, and for the resumption of the jaghires, he expresses to the Nabob the warm and lively interest which he took in his welfare, the sincerity and ardor of his friendship, and that, tho his presence was eminently wanted at Calcutta, he could not refrain from coming to his assistance, and that in the meantime he had sent four regiments to his aid. So deliberate and cool, so hypocritical and insinuating is the villainy of this man! What heart is not exasperated by the malignity of a treachery so barefaced and dispassionate? At length, however, the Nabob was on his guard. He could not be deceived by this mask. The offer of the four regiments developed to him the object of Mr. Hastings. He perceived the dagger bunglingly concealed in the hand which was treacherously extended as if to his assistance. From this moment the last faint ray of hope expired in his bosom. We accordingly find no further confidence of the Nabob in the prisoner. Mr. Middleton now swayed his iron scepter without control. The jaghires were seized. Every measure was carried. The Nabob, mortified, humbled, and degraded, sunk into insignificance and contempt.

This letter was sent at the very time when the troops surrounded the walls of Fyzabad; and then began a scene of horrors, which, if I wished to inflame your lordship's feelings, I should only have occasion minutely to describe; to state the violence committed on that palace which the piety of the kingdom had raised for the retreat and seclusion of the objects of its pride and veneration! It was in these shades, rendered sacred by superstition, that innocence reposed. Here venerable age and helpless infancy found an asylum! If we look, my lords, into the whole of this most wicked transaction, from the time when this treachery was first conceived, to that when, by a series of artifices the most execrable, it was brought to a completion, the prisoner will be seen standing aloof, indeed, but not inactive. He will be discovered reviewing his agents, rebuking at one time the pale con-

science of Middleton, at another, relying on the
stouter villainy of Hyder Beg Cawn. With
all the calmness of veteran delinquency, his eye
will be seen ranging through the busy prospect,
piercing the darkness of subordinate guilt, and
disciplining with congenial adroitness the agents
of his crimes and the instruments of his cruelty.

The feelings, my lords, of the several parties
at the time will be most properly judged of by
their respective correspondence. When the Bow
Begum, despairing of redress from the Nabob,
addressed herself to Mr. Middleton, and remind-
ed him of the guarantee which he had signed,
she was instantly promised that the amount of
her jaghire should be made good, tho he
said he could not interfere with the sovereign
decision of the Nabob respecting the lands. The
deluded and unfortunate woman "thanked God
that Mr. Middleton was at hand for her relief."
At this very instant he was directing every effort to her destruction. For he had actually
written the orders which were to take the collection out of the hands of her agents! But let it
not be forgotten, my lords, when the Begum
was undeceived, when she found that British
faith was no protection, when she found that
she should leave the country, and prayed to the
God of nations not to grant his peace to those
who remained behind, there was still no charge
of rebellion, no recrimination made to all her
approaches for the broken faith to the English.
That when stung to madness, she asked "how

long would be her reign," there was no mention of her disaffection. The stress is therefore idle, which the counsel for the prisoner have strove to lay on these expressions of an injured and enraged woman. When at last irritated beyond bearing, she denounced infamy on the heads of her oppressors, who is there that will not say that she spoke in a prophetic spirit; and that what she then predicted has not even to its last letter been accomplished? But did Mr. Middleton even to this violence retort any particle of accusation? No. He sent a jocose reply, stating that he had received such a letter under her seal, but that from its contents he could not suspect it to come from her, and begged therefore that she would endeavor to detect the forgery. Thus did he add to foul injuries the vile aggravation of a brutal jest. Like the tiger, he showed the savageness of his nature by grinning at his prey and fawning over the last agonies of his unfortunate victim.

The letters, my lords, were then enclosed to the Nabob, who no more than the rest made any attempt to justify himself by imputing any criminality to the Begums. He only sighed a hope that his conduct to his parents had drawn no shame upon his head; and declared his intention to punish not any disaffection in the Begums, but some officious servants who had dared to foment the misunderstanding between them and himself. A letter was finally sent to Mr. Hastings, about six days before the seizure of the treasures from the Begums, declaring their innocence, and referring the governor-general in proof of it to Captain Gordon, whose life they had protected, and whose safety should have been their justification. This inquiry was never made. It was looked on as unnecessary, because the conviction of their innocence was too deeply impressed already.

The counsel, my lords, in recommending an attention to the public in preference to the private letters, remarked particularly. that one of the latter should not be taken in evidence, because it was evidently and abstractedly private, relating the anxieties of Mr. Middleton, on account of the illness of his son. This is a singular argument indeed. The circumstance, however, undoubtedly merits strict observation, tho not in the view in which it was placed by the counsel. It goes to show that some at least of the persons concerned in these transactions felt the force of those rites which their efforts were directed to tear asunder; that those who could ridicule the respective attachment of a mother and a son; who could prohibit the reverence of the son to the mother; who could deny to maternal debility the protection which filial tenderness should afford, were yet sensible of the straining of those chords by which they are connected. There is something in the present business, with all that is horrible to create aversion so vilely loathsome, as to excite disgust.

It is, my lords, surely superfluous to dwell on

the sacredness of the ties which those aliens to
feeling, those apostates to humanity thus divided. In such an assembly as the one before
which I speak there is not an eye but must look
reproof to this conduct, not a heart but must
anticipate its condemnation. Filial piety! It is
the primal bond of society. It is that instinctive
principle, which, panting for its proper good,
soothes, unbidden, each sense and sensibility of
man. It now quivers on every lip. It now
beams from every eye. It is that gratitude
which, softening under the sense of recollected
good, is eager to own the vast, countless debt it
never, alas! can pay, for so many long years of
unceasing solicitudes, honorable self-denials, life-
preserving cares. It is that part of our practise where duty drops its awe, where reverence
refines into love. It asks no aid of memory.
It needs not the deductions of reason. Pre-
existing, paramount over all, whether moral
law or human rule, few arguments can increase
and none can diminish it. It is the sacrament
of our nature; not only the duty, but the indulgence of man. It is his first great privilege. It
is among his last most endearing delights. It
causes the bosom to glow with reverberated love.
It requites the visitations of nature, and returns
the blessings that have been received. It fires
emotion into vital principle. It changes what
was instinct into a master passion, sways all the
sweetest energies of man, hangs over each vicis-
situde of all that must pass away; aids the melan-

choly virtues in their last sad tasks of life; cheers the languors of decrepitude and age; "explores the thought, explains the aching eye!"

But, my lords, I am ashamed to consume so much of your lordships' time in attempting to give a cold picture of this sacred impulse when I behold so many breathing testimonies of its influence around me; when every countenance in this assembly is beaming and erecting itself into the recognition of this universal principle!

The expressions contained in the letter of Mr. Middleton, of tender solicitude for his son, have been also mentioned as a proof of the amiableness of his affections. I confess that they do not tend to raise his character in my estimation. Is it not rather an aggravation of his guilt that he, who thus felt the anxieties of a parent, and who consequently must be sensible of the reciprocal feelings of a child, could be brought to tear asunder, and violate in others, all those dear and sacred bonds? Does it not enhance the turpitude of the transaction that it was not the result of idiotic ignorance or brutal indifference? I aver that his guilt is increased and magnified by these considerations. His criminality would have been less had he been insensible to tenderness, less if he had not been so thoroughly acquainted with the true quality of parental love and filial duty.

The jaghires being seized, my lords, the Begums were left without the smallest share of that pecuniary compensation promised by Mr.

Middleton, as an equivalent for the resumption;
and as when tyranny and injustice take the
field, they are always attended by their camp
followers, paltry pilfering and petty insult; so
in this instance, the goods taken from the princesses were sold at a mock sale at an inferior
value. Even gold and jewels, to use the language of the Begums, instantly lost their value
when it was known that they came from them.
Their ministers were imprisoned to extort the
deficiency which this fraud occasioned, and
every mean art was employed to justify a continuance of cruelty toward them. Yet this was
small to the frauds of Mr. Hastings. After ex-
torting upward of £600,000, he forbade Mr.
Middleton to come to a conclusive settlement
with the princesses. He knew that the treasons
of our allies in India had their origin solely in
the wants of the company. He could not therefore say that the Begums were entirely innocent
until he had consulted the General Record of
Crimes, the Cash Account of Calcutta! His
prudence was fully justified by the event. For
there was actually found a balance of twenty-
six lacks more against the Begums, which £260,-
000 worth of treason had never been dreamed of
before. "Talk not to us," said the governor-general, "of their guilt or innocence, but as it suits
the company's credit! We will not try them
by the Code of Justinian, nor the Institutes of
Timur. We will not judge them either by the
British laws or their local customs! No! We

will try them by the multiplication table; we will
find them guilty by the Rule of Three; and we
will condemn them according to the unerring
rules of—Cocker's Arithmetic!"[1]

My lords, the prisoner has said in his defense
that the cruelties exercised toward the Begums
were not of his order. But in another part of
it he avows, "that whatever were their distresses,
and whoever was the agent in the measure, it
was, in his opinion, reconcilable to justice, honor,
and sound policy."

By the testimony of Major Scott it appears,
that tho the defense of the prisoner was not
drawn up by himself, yet that this paragraph
he wrote with his own proper hand. Middleton,
it seems, had confessed his share in these transactions with some degree of compunction, and
solicitude as to the consequences. The prisoner
observing it, cries out to him: Give me the pen;
I will defend the measure as just and necessary! I will take something upon myself. Whatever part of the load you can not bear, my
unburdened character shall assume. Your conduct I will crown with my irresistible approbation. Do you find memory and I will find character; and thus twin warriors we will go into
the field, each in his proper sphere of action,

---

[1] "Cocker's Arithmetic, being a plain and easy method, composed
by Edward Cocker, perused and published by John Hankins, writing master, by the author's correct copy," was published in 1678,
three years after Cocker's death, and is believed to have gone
through 112 editions, including Scotch and Irish.

and assault, repulse, and contumely shall all be set at defiance.

If I could not prove, my lords, that those acts of Mr. Middleton were in reality the acts of Mr. Hastings, I should not trouble your lordships by combating them. But as this part of his criminality can be incontestably ascertained, I appeal to the assembled legislators of this realm, to say, whether these acts were justifiable on the score of policy. I appeal to all the august presidents in the courts of British justice, and to all the learned ornaments of the profession, to decide whether these acts were reconcilable to justice. I appeal to the reverend assemblage of prelates feeling for the general interests of humanity, and for the honor of the religion to which they belong, to determine whether these acts of Mr. Hastings and Mr. Middleton were such as a Christian ought to perform or a man to avow.

My lords, with the ministers of the Nabob, Bahar Ally Cawn and Jewar Ally Cawn, was confined in the same prison that arch rebel Sumshire Cawn, against whom so much criminality has been charged by the counsel for the prisoner. We hear, however, of no inquiry having been made concerning his treason, tho so many were held respecting the treasures of the others. With all his guilt, he was not so far noticed as to be deprived of his food, to be complimented with fetters, or even to have the satisfaction of being scourged; but was cruelly liberated from a dungeon and ignominiously let loose on his parole! The Begums' ministers, on the contrary, to extort from them the disclosure of the place which concealed the treasures, were, according to the evidence of Mr. Holt, after being fettered and imprisoned, led out on a scaffold, and this array of terrors proving unavailing, the meek-tempered Middleton, as a dernier resort, menaced them with a confinement in the fortress of Chunargar. Thus, my lords, was a British garrison made the climax of cruelties!

To English arms, to English officers around whose banners Humanity has ever entwined her most glorious wreath, how will this sound? It was in this fort, where the British flag was flying, that these helpless prisoners were doomed to deeper dungeons, heavier chains, and severer punishments. Where that flag was displayed, which was wont to cheer the depressed, and to dilate the subdued heart of misery, these venerable, but unfortunate men were fated to encounter every aggravation of horror and distress. It, moreover, appears that they were both cruelly flogged, tho one was above seventy years of age. Being charged with disaffection, they vindicated their innocence. "Tell us where are the remaining treasures," was the reply. "It is only a treachery to your immediate sovereigns, and you will then be fit associates for the representatives of British faith and British justice in India!"

O Faith! O Justice! I conjure you by your

sacred names to depart for a moment from this place, tho it be your peculiar residence; nor hear your names profaned by such a sacrilegious combination as that which I am now compelled to repeat! where all the fair forms of nature and art, truth and peace, policy and horror, shrink back aghast from the deleterious shade where all existences, nefarious and vile, have sway—where we see amid black agents on one side and Middleton with Impey on the other, the great figure of the piece—characteristic in his place, aloof and independent from the puny profligacy in his train, but far from idle and inactive, turning a malignant eye on all mischief that awaits him; the multiplied apparatus of temporizing expedients and intimidating instruments, now cringing on his prey and fawning on his vengeance—now quickening the limping pace of craft, and forcing every stand that retiring nature can make to the heart; the attachments and the decorums of life; each emotion of tenderness and honor; and all the distinctions of national pride; with a long catalog of crimes and aggravations, beyond the reach of thought for human malignity to perpetrate, or human vengeance to punish; lower than perdition—blacker than despair!

It might, my lords, have been hoped, for the honor of the human heart, that the Begums were themselves exempted from a share in these sufferings, and that they had been wounded only through the sides of their ministers. The reverse of this, however, is the fact. Their palace was surrounded by a guard, which was withdrawn by Major Gilpin, to avoid the growing resentments of the people, and replaced by Mr. Middleton, through the fears of that "dreadful responsibility" which was imposed on him by Mr. Hastings. The women, also, of the Khord Mahal, who were not involved in the Begums' supposed crimes; who had raised no sub-rebellion of their own; and who, it has been proved, lived in a distinct dwelling, were causelessly implicated, nevertheless, in the same punishment. Their residence being surrounded with guards, they were driven to despair by famine, and when they poured forth in sad procession, were beaten with bludgeons and forced back by the soldiery to the scene of madness which they had quitted. These are acts, my lords, which, when told, need no comment. I will not offer a single syllable to awaken your lordships' feelings, but leave it to the facts which have been stated, to make their own impression.

The inquiry which now only remains, my lords, is, whether Mr. Hastings is to be answerable for the crimes committed by his agents? It has been fully proved that Mr. Middleton signed the treaty with the superior Begum in October, 1778. He also acknowledged signing some others of a different date, but could not recollect the authority by which he did it. These treaties were recognized by Mr. Hastings, as appears by the evidence of Mr. Purling, in the year 1780. In that of October, 1778, the jaghire

was secured, which was allotted for the support
of the women in the Khord Mahal. But still
the prisoner pleads that he is not accountable
for the cruelties which were exercised. His is
the plea which Tyranny, aided by its prime
minister, Treachery, is always sure to set up.
Mr. Middleton has attempted to strengthen this
ground by endeavoring to claim the whole infamy in those transactions, and to monopolize
the guilt! He dared even to aver that he had
been condemned by Mr. Hastings for the ignominious part he had acted. He dared to avow
this because Mr. Hastings was on his trial and
he thought he never would be arraigned. But,
in the face of this court, and before he left the
bar he was compelled to confess that it was for
the lenience and not the severity of his proceedings that he had been reproved by the prisoner.

It will not, I trust, be concluded that, because
Mr. Hastings has not marked every passing
shade of guilt, and because he has only given
the bold outline of cruelty, he is therefore to be
acquitted. It is laid down by the law of England, that law which is the perfection of reason,
that a person ordering an act to be done by his
agent is answerable for that act with all its
consequences. *Quid facit per alium, facit per
se.* Middleton was appointed in 1777 the confidential agent—the second self of Mr. Hastings. The governor-general ordered the measure.
Even if he never saw, nor heard afterward of

its consequences, he was therefore answerable for every pang that was inflicted, and for all the blood that was shed. But he did hear, and that instantly, of the whole. He wrote to accuse Middleton of forbearance and of neglect! He commanded him to work upon the hopes and fears of the princesses, and to leave no means untried, until, to speak his own language, which was better suited to the banditti of a cavern, "he obtained possession of the secret hoards of the old ladies." He would not allow even of a delay of two days to smooth the compelled approaches of a son to his mother on this occasion! His orders were peremptory. After this, my lords, can it be said, that the prisoner was ignorant of the acts, or not culpable for their consequences? It is true, he did not direct the guards, the famine, and the bludgeons; he did not weigh the fetters, nor number the lashes to be inflicted on his victims; but yet he is equally guilty as if he had born an active and personal share in each transaction. It is as if he had commanded that the heart should be torn from the bosom, and enjoined that no blood should follow. He is in the same degree accountable to the law, to his country, to his conscience, and to his God.

The prisoner has endeavored also to get rid of a part of his guilt by observing that he was but one of the supreme council, and that all the rest had sanctioned those transactions with their approbation. Even if it were true that others did participate in the guilt, it can not tend to diminish his criminality. But the fact is that the council erred in nothing so much as in a reprehensible credulity given to the declarations of the governor-general. They knew not a word of those transactions until they were finally concluded. It was not until the January following that they saw the mass of falsehood which had been published under the title of "Mr. Hastings's Narrative." They were then unaccountably duped to permit a letter to pass, dated the 29th of November, intended to seduce the directors into a belief that they had received intelligence at that time, which was not the fact. These observations, my lords, are not meant to cast any obloquy on the council. They undoubtedly were deceived, and the deceit practised on them is a decided proof of his conscious ness of guilt. When tired of corporal infliction, Mr. Hastings was gratified by insulting the understanding. The coolness and reflection with which this act was managed and concerted, raises its enormity and blackens its turpitude. It proves the prisoner to be that monster in nature, a deliberate and reasoning tyrant! Other tyrants of whom we read, such as a Nero or a Caligula, were urged to their crimes by the impetuosity of passion. High rank disqualified them from advice, and perhaps equally prevented reflection. But in the prisoner, we have a man born in a state of mediocrity; bred to mercantile life; used to system and accustomed to regularity; who was accountable to his masters, and therefore was compelled to think and to deliberate on every part of his conduct. It is this cool deliberation, I say, which renders his crimes more horrible and his character more atrocious.

When, my lords, the board of directors received the advices which Mr. Hastings thought proper to transmit, tho unfurnished with any other materials to form their judgment, they expressed very strongly their doubts, and properly ordered an inquiry into the circumstances of the alleged disaffection of the Begums, declaring it at the same time to be a debt which was due to the honor and justice of the British nation. This inquiry, however, Mr. Hastings thought it absolutely necessary to elude. He stated to the council, in answer, that it would revive those animosities that subsisted between the Begums and the Visier which had then subsided. If the former were inclined to appeal to a foreign jurisdiction, "they were the best judges of their own feeling, and should be left to make their own complaint." All this, however, my lords, is nothing to the magnificent paragraph which concludes this communication. "Besides," says he, "I hope it will not be a departure from official language to say that the majesty of justice ought not to be approached without solicitation. She ought not to descend to inflame or provoke, but to withhold her judgment, until she is called on to determine." What is still more astonishing is that Sir John Macpherson, who, tho a man of sense and honor, is rather oriental in his imagination, and not learned in the sublime and beautiful from the immortal leader of this prosecution, was caught by this bold, bombastic quibble, and joined in the same words, "that the majesty of justice ought not to be approached without solicitation." But, my lords, do you, the judges of this land, and the expounders of its rightful laws, do you approve of this mockery, and call it the character of justice, which takes the form of right to excite wrong? No, my lords, justice is not this halt and miserable object; it is not the ineffective bauble of an Indian pagod; it is not the portentous phantom of despair; it is not like any fabled monster, formed in the eclipse of reason, and found in some unhallowed grove of superstitious darkness and political dismay! No, my lords. In the happy reverse of all this, I turn from the disgusting caricature to the real image! Justice I have now before me, august and pure! the abstract idea of all that would be perfect in the spirits and the aspirings of men! where the mind rises, where the heart expands; where the countenance is ever placid and benign; where her favorite attitude is to stoop to the unfortunate; to hear their cry and to help them; to rescue and relieve, to succor and save; majestic, from its mercy; venerable, from its utility; uplifted, without pride; firm, without obduracy; beneficent in each preference; lovely, tho in her frown!

On that justice I rely; deliberate and sure, abstracted from all party purpose and political speculation, not on words, but on facts. You, my lords, who hear me, I conjure, by those rights it is your best privilege to preserve; by that fame it is your best pleasure to inherit; by all those feelings which refer to the first term in the series of existence, the original compact of our nature—our controlling rank in the creation. This is the call on all to administer to truth and equity, as they would satisfy the laws and satisfy themselves, with the most exalted bliss possible or conceivable for our nature —the self-approving consciousness of virtue— when the condemnation we look for will be one of the most ample mercies accomplished for mankind since the creation of the world! My lords, I have done.

CURRAN

I

IN BEHALF OF ROWAN AND FREE SPEECH [1]

(1794)

Born in 1750, died in 1817; admitted to the Irish Bar in 1775; entered
the Irish Parliament in 1783; defended prisoners arrested during the
Irish Insurrection of 1798; Master of the Rolls in Ireland in 1806-14.

WHEN I consider the period at which this
prosecution is brought forward; when I behold
the extraordinary safeguard of armed soldiers,
resorted to, no doubt, for the preservation of
peace and order; when I catch, as I can not but
do, the throb of public anxiety, which beats
from one end to the other of this hall; when
I reflect on what may be the fate of a man
of the most beloved personal character, of one of

[1] Archibald Hamilton Rowan was secretary of the Dublin Society
of United Irishmen. In August, 1792, in reply to a proclamation
against "the Volunteers of Ireland," Rowan had published an address inviting them to resume their arms. The government having
decided to prosecute him, Curran in 1794 was engaged to defend
him. It was in this case that Curran began a series of defenses in
state trials which form the chief basis of his fame as an orator.
The full report of his speech in defense of Rowan fills twenty-five
large pages in small type. It was delivered "from a dozen catch-
words on the back of his brief." Soldiers in the court-room frequently interrupted him with threats. On leaving the court-room,
Curran's horses were taken from his carriage and the carriage
dragged to his home by his admirers. Rowan, convicted and sentenced to imprisonment, escaped to France.

the most respected families of our country—
himself the only individual of that family—I
may almost say of that country: who can look
to that possible fate with unconcern? Feeling,
as I do, all these impressions, it is in the honest
simplicity of my heart I speak, when I say that
I never rose in a court of justice with so much
embarrassment as upon this occasion.

If, gentlemen, I could entertain a hope of
finding refuge for the disconcertion of my mind
in the perfect composure of yours, if I could
suppose that those awful vicissitudes of human
events, which have been stated or alluded to,
could leave your judgments undisturbed and
your hearts at ease, I know I should form a most
erroneous opinion of your character. I entertain no such chimerical hopes; I form no such
unworthy opinions; I expect not that your
hearts can be more at ease than my own. I have
no right to expect; but I have a right to call
upon you in the name of your country, in the
name of the living God, of whose eternal justice
you are now administering that portion which
dwells with us on this side of the grave, to discharge your breasts, as far as you are able, of
every bias of prejudice or passion; that if my
client is guilty of the offense charged upon him
you may give tranquillity to the public by a
firm verdict of conviction; or if he is innocent,
by as firm a verdict of acquittal; and that you
will do this in defiance of the paltry artifices and
senseless clamors that have been resorted to in

order to bring him to his trial with anticipated conviction.

The peculiarity of the British Constitution (to which, in its fullest extent, we have an undoubted right, however distant we may be from the actual enjoyment, and in which it surpasses every known government in Europe) is this: that its only professed object is the general good, and its only foundation the general will. Hence the people have a right, acknowledged from time immemorial, fortified by a pile of statutes, and authenticated by a revolution that speaks louder than them all, to see whether abuses have been committed, and whether their properties and their liberties have been attended to as they ought to be. This is a kind of subject which I feel myself overawed when I approach. There are certain fundamental principles which nothing but necessity should expose to a public examination. They are pillars the depth of whose foundation you can not explore without endangering their strength; but let it be recollected that the discussion of such topics should not be condemned in me nor visited upon my client. The blame, if any there be, should rest only with those who have forced them into discussion. I say, therefore, it is the right of the people to keep an eternal watch upon the conduct of their rulers; and in order to do that, the freedom of the Press has been cherished by the law of England. In private defamation let it never be tolerated; in wicked and wanton aspersion upon a good and honest administration let it never be supported—not that a good government can be exposed to danger by groundless accusation, but because a bad government is sure to find in the detected falsehood of a licentious Press a security and a credit which it could never otherwise obtain.

Gentlemen, without any observation of mine, you must see that this indictment contains a direct charge upon Mr. Rowan; namely, that he did, with the intents set forth in the information, publish this paper, so that here you have, in fact, two or three questions for your decision: first, the matter of fact of the publication; namely, did Mr. Rowan publish that paper? If Mr. Rowan did not, in fact, publish that paper, you have no longer any question on which to employ your minds. If you think that he was in fact the publisher, then, and not till then, arises the great and important subject to which your judgments must be directed. And that comes shortly and simply to this: Is the paper a libel; and did he publish it with the intent charged in the information?

But whatever you may think of the abstract question, whether the paper be libelous or not, and of which paper it has not even been insinuated that he is the author, there can be no ground for a verdict against him unless you also are persuaded that what he did was done with a criminal design. I wish, gentlemen, to simplify, and not to perplex; I therefore say

again, if these three circumstances conspire—
that he published it, that it was a libel, and that
it was published with the purposes alleged in
the information—you ought unquestionably to
find him guilty; if, on the other hand, you do
not find that all these circumstances concurred;
if you can not, upon your oaths, say that he
published it; if it be not in your opinion a
libel; and if he did not publish it with the intention alleged; I say upon the failure of any
one of these points my client is entitled, in justice
and upon your oaths, to a verdict of acquittal.

Gentlemen, Mr. Attorney-General has thought
proper to direct your attention to the state and
circumstances of public affairs at the time of
this transaction; let me also make a few retro-
spective observations on a period at which he
has but slightly glanced; I speak of the events
which took place before the close of the American war. You know, gentlemen, that France had
espoused the cause of America, and we became
thereby engaged in war with that nation. *"Heu
nescia mens hominum futuri!"*

Little did that ill-fated monarch know that
he was forming the first causes of those disastrous events that were to end in the subver-
sion of his throne, in the slaughter of his family,
and the deluging of his country with the blood
of his people. You can not but remember that
at a time when we had scarcely a regular soldier
for our defense, when the old and the young
were alarmed and terrified with the apprehen-

sion of invasion, Providence seemed to have worked a sort of miracle in our favor.

You saw a band of armed men come forth at the great call of nature, of honor, and their country. You saw men of the greatest wealth and rank; you saw every class of the community give up its members and send them armed into the field to protect the public and private tranquillity of Ireland. It is impossible for any man to turn back to that period without reviving those sentiments of tenderness and gratitude which then beat in the public bosom; to recollect amid what applause, what tears, what prayers, what benedictions, they walked forth among spectators agitated by the mingled sensations of terror and reliance, of danger and protection, imploring the blessings of Heaven upon their heads and its conquest upon their swords. That illustrious and adored and abused body of men stood forward and assumed the title which I trust the ingratitude of their country will never blot from its history—"The Volunteers of Ireland."

Give me leave, now, with great respect, to put one question to you: Do you think the assembling of that glorious band of patriots was an insurrection? Do you think the invitation to that assembling would have been sedition? They came under no commission but the call of their country; unauthorized and unsanctioned except by public emergency and public danger. I ask: Was that meeting an insurrec-

tion or not? I put another question: If any
man had then published a call on that body,
and stated that war was declared against the
State; that the regular troops were withdrawn;
that our coasts were hovered round by the ships
of the enemy; that the moment was approaching when the unprotected feebleness of age and
sex, when the sanctity of habitation, would be
disregarded and profaned by the brutal ferocity
of a rude invader: if any man had then said to
them, "Leave your industry for a while, that
you may return to it again, and come forth in
arms for the public defense,"—I put this question boldly to you, gentlemen,—it is not the case
of the volunteers of that day; it is the case
of my client at this hour, which I put to you,—
would that call have been then pronounced in
a court of justice, or by a jury on their oaths,
a criminal and seditious invitation to insurrection? If it would not have been so then, upon
what principle can it be so now? What is the
force and perfection of the law?

It is a question, gentlemen, upon which you
only can decide; it is for you to say whether it
was criminal in the defendant to be so misled,
and whether he is to fall a sacrifice to
the prosecution of that government by which
he was so deceived. I say again, gentlemen, you can look only to his own words as the
interpreter of his meaning, and to the state and
circumstances of his country, as he was made
to believe them, as the clue to his intention. The

case, then, gentlemen, is shortly and simply this: A man of the first family and fortune and character and property among you reads a proclamation stating the country to be in danger from abroad and at home, and thus alarmed—thus upon authority of the prosecutor alarmed—applies to that august body before whose awful presence sedition must vanish and insurrection disappear.

You must surrender, I hesitate not to say it, your oaths to unfounded assertion, if you can submit to say that such an act of such a man, so warranted, is a wicked and seditious libel. If he was a dupe, let me ask you who was the impostor? I blush and I shrink with shame and detestation from that meanness of dupery and servile complaisance which could make that dupe a victim to the accusation of that impostor.

You perceive, gentlemen, that I am going into the merits of this publication before I apply myself to the question which is first in order of time—namely, whether the publication, in point of fact, is to be ascribed to Mr. Rowan or not. I have been unintentionally led into this violation of order. I should effect no purpose of either brevity or clearness by returning to the more methodical course of observation. I have been naturally drawn from it by the superior importance of the topic I am upon—namely, the merit of the publication in question.

This publication, if ascribable at all to Mr. Rowan, contains four distinct subjects. The

first, the invitation to the volunteers to arm.
Upon that I have already observed; but those
that remain are surely of much importance, and
no doubt are prosecuted as equally criminal.
The paper next states the necessity of a reform
in Parliament; it states, thirdly, the necessity of
an emancipation of the Catholic inhabitants of
Ireland; and, as necessary to the achievement
of all these objects, does, fourthly, state the necessity of a general delegated convention of the
people.

Be pleased now, gentlemen, to consider whether
the statement of the imperfection in your
representation has been made with a desire
of inflaming an attack upon the public tranquillity or with an honest purpose of procuring
a remedy for an actually existing grievance. It
is impossible not to revert to the situation of
the times; and let me remind you, that whatever observations of this kind I am compelled
thus to make in a court of justice, the uttering
of them in this place is not imputable to my
client, but to the necessity of defense imposed
upon him by this extraordinary prosecution.

Gentlemen, the representation of your people
is the vital principle of their political existence.
Without it they are dead, or they live only to
servitude; without it there are two estates acting
upon and against the third, instead of acting in
cooperation with it; without it, if the people
are oppressed by their judges, where is the tribunal to which their judges can be amenable?

Without it, if they are trampled upon and plundered by a minister, where is the tribunal to which the offender shall be amenable? Without it, where is the ear to hear, or the heart to feel, or the hand to redress their sufferings? Shall they be found, let me ask you, in the accursed bands of imps and minions that bask in their disgrace, and fatten upon their spoils, and flourish upon their ruin? But let me not put this to you as a merely speculative question. It is a plain question of fact: rely upon it, physical man is everywhere the same; it is only the various operations of moral causes that give variety to the social or individual character and condition. How otherwise happens it that modern slavery looks quietly at the despot on the very spot where Leonidas expired? The answer is easy; Sparta has not changed her climate, but she has lost that government which her liberty could not survive.

I call you, therefore, to the plain question of fact. This paper recommends a reform in Parliament: I put that question to your consciences; do you think it needs that reform? I put it boldly and fairly to you; do you think the people of Ireland are represented as they ought to be?

Do you hesitate for an answer? If you do, let me remind you that until the last year three millions of your countrymen have, by the express letter of the law, been excluded from the reality of actual, and even from the phantom of virtual representation. Shall we, then, be told that this is only the affirmation of a wicked and seditious incendiary? If you do not feel the mockery of such a charge, look at your country; in what state do you find it? Is it in a state of tranquillity and general satisfaction? These are traces by which good are ever to be distinguished from bad governments without any very minute inquiry or speculative refinement. Do you feel that a veneration for the law, a pious and humble attachment to the Constitution, form the political morality of the people? Do you find that comfort and competency among your people which are always to be found where a government is mild and moderate, where taxes are imposed by a body who have an interest in treating the poorer orders with compassion, and preventing the weight of taxation from pressing sore upon them?

Gentlemen, I mean not to impeach the state of your representation; I am not saying that it is defective or that it ought to be altered or amended; nor is this a place for me to say whether I think that three millions of the inhabitants of a country whose whole number is but four ought to be admitted to any efficient situation in the state.

It may be said, and truly, that these are not questions for either of us directly to decide; but you can not refuse them some passing consideration at least when you remember that on this subject the real question for your decision is whether the allegation of a defect in your Constitution is so utterly unfounded and false that you can ascribe it only to the malice and perverseness of a wicked mind and not to the innocent mistake of an ordinary understanding; whether it may not be a mistake; whether it can be only sedition.

And here, gentlemen, I own I can not but regret that one of our countrymen should be criminally pursued for asserting the necessity of a reform at the very moment when that necessity seems admitted by the Parliament itself; that this unhappy reform shall at the same moment be a subject of legislative discussion and criminal prosecution.

Far am I from imputing any sinister design to the virtue or wisdom of our government; but who can avoid feeling the deplorable impression that must be made on the public mind when the demand for that reform is answered by a criminal information! I am the more forcibly impressed by this consideration when I consider that when this information was first put on the file the subject was transiently mentioned in the House of Commons.

This paper, gentlemen, insists upon the necessity of emancipating the Catholics of Ireland, and that is charged as a part of the libel. If they had kept this prosecution impending for another year, how much would remain for a jury to decide upon, I should be at a loss to discover. It seems as if the progress of public reformation was eating away the ground of the prosecution. Since the commencement of the prosecution this part of the libel has unluckily received the sanction of the Legislature. In that interval our Catholic brethren have obtained that admission which it seems it was a libel to propose. In what way to account for this I am really at a loss.

Have any alarms been occasioned by the emancipation of our Catholic brethren? Has the bigoted malignity of any individuals been crushed? Or has the stability of the government or has that of the country been weakened? Or are one million of subjects stronger than three millions? Do you think that the benefit they received should be poisoned by the stings of vengeance? If you think so you must say to them: "You have demanded your emancipation and you have got it; but we abhor your persons, we are outraged at your success, and we will stigmatize by a criminal prosecution the relief which you have obtained from the voice of your country."

I ask you, gentlemen, do you think, as honest men anxious for the public tranquillity, conscious that there are wounds not yet completely cicatrized, that you ought to speak this language at this time to men who are too much disposed to think that in this very emancipation they have been saved from their own Parliament by the humanity of their sovereign? Or do you wish to prepare them for the revocation of these improvident concessions? Do you think it wise or humane at this moment to insult them by sticking up in a pillory the man who dared to stand forth their advocate?

I put it to your oaths, do you think that a blessing of that kind, that a victory obtained by justice over bigotry and oppression, should have a stigma cast upon it by an ignominious sentence upon men bold and honest enough to propose that measure; to propose the redeeming of religion from the abuses of the Church, the reclaiming of three millions of men from bondage, and giving liberty to all who had a right to demand it—giving, I say, in the so-much-censured words of this paper, "Universal Emancipation?"

I speak in the spirit of the British law, which makes liberty commensurate with and inseparable from the British soil; which proclaims, even to the stranger and the sojourner, the moment he sets his foot upon British earth, that the ground on which he treads is holy and consecrated by the genius of universal emancipation.

No matter in what language his doom may have been pronounced; no matter what complexion incompatible with freedom an Indian or an African sun may have burned upon him; no matter in what disastrous battle his liberty may have been cloven down; no matter with what solemnities he may have been devoted upon the altar of slavery; the first moment he touches the sacred soil of Britain the altar and the god sink together in the dust; his soul walks abroad in her

own majesty; his body swells beyond the measure of his chains that burst from around him,
and he stands redeemed, regenerated, and dis-
enthraled by the irresistible genius of universal
emancipation.[1]

Gentlemen, I am not such a fool as to ascribe
any effusion of this sort to any merit of mine.
It is the mighty theme, and not the inconsiderable advocate, that can excite interest in the
hearer. What you hear is but the testimony
which nature bears to her own character; it is
the effusion of her gratitude to that Power
which stamped that character. And, gentlemen,
permit me to say that if my client had occasion
to defend his cause by any mad or drunken
appeals to extravagance or licentiousness, I trust
in God I stand in such a situation that, humble
as I am, he would not have resorted to me to be
his advocate. It was not recommended to his
choice by any connection of principle or party,
or even private friendship; and, saying this, I
can not but add that I consider not to be acquainted with such a man as Mr. Rowan a want
of personal good fortune.

Gentlemen, upon this great subject of reform
and emancipation there is a latitude and boldness of remark, justifiable in the people, and

---

[1] It is recorded that at this point Curran was interrupted by
a sudden burst of applause. Silence was finally restored by
Lord Clonmel, who acknowledged the pleasure he had himself felt
at the brilliant display of professional talent, but disapproved of
intemperate expressions of applause in courts of justice.

necessary to the defense of Mr. Rowan, for which the habits of professional studies and technical adherence to established forms have rendered me unfit.

Gentlemen, you are sitting in a country that has a right to the British Constitution, and which is bound by an indissoluble union with the British nation. If you were now even at liberty to debate upon that subject—if you even were not by the most solemn compacts, founded upon the authority of your ancestors and of yourselves, bound to that alliance, and had an election now to make, in the present unhappy state of Europe—if you had heretofore been a stranger to Great Britain, you would now say, we will enter into society and union with you:

> "Commune periculum,
> Una salus ambobus erit."

But to accomplish that union, let me tell you, you must learn to become like the English people: it is vain to say you will protect their freedom if you abandon your own. The pillar whose base has no foundation can give no support to the dome under which its head is placed; and if you profess to give England that assistance which you refuse to yourselves she will laugh at your folly and despise your meanness and insincerity.

I know you will interpret what I say with the candor in which it is spoken. England is marked by a natural avarice of freedom which she is studious to engross and accumulate, but most unwilling to impart, whether from any necessity of policy, or from her weakness, or from her pride, I will not presume to say; but that so is the fact you need not look to the east or to the west—you need only look to yourselves.

In order to confirm that observation I would appeal to what fell from the learned counsel for the Crown, that, notwithstanding the alliance subsisting for two centuries past between the two countries, the date of liberty in one goes no further back than the year 1784. If it required additional confirmation I should state the case of the invaded American and the subjugated Indian to prove that the policy of England has ever been to govern her connections more as colonies than allies; and it must be owing to the great spirit, indeed, of Ireland, if she shall continue free. Rely upon it, she will ever have to hold her course against an adverse current; rely upon it, if the popular spring does not continue firm and elastic, a short interval of debilitated nerve and broken force will send you down the stream again and reconsign you to the condition of a province.

If such should become the fate of your Constitution, ask yourselves what must be the motive of your government? It is easier to govern a province by a faction than to govern a coordinate country by coordinate means. I do not say it is now, but it will be always thought easiest by the managers of the day to govern the Irish nation by the agency of such a faction as long as this country shall be found willing to let her connection with Great Britain be preserved only by her own degradation. In such a precarious and wretched state of things, if it shall ever be found to exist, the true friend of Irish liberty and British connection will see that the only means of saving both must be, as Lord Chatham expressed it, "the infusion of new health and blood into the Constitution."

He will see how deep a stake each country has in the liberty of the other; he will see what a bulwark he adds to the common cause by giving England a coordinate and cointerested ally instead of an oppressed, enfeebled, and suspected dependent; he will see how grossly the credulity of Britain is abused by those who make her believe that her solid interest is promoted by our depression; he will see the desperate precipice to which she approaches by such a conduct, and with an animated and generous piety he will labor to avert her danger.

But, gentlemen of the jury, what is likely to be his fate? The interest of the sovereign must be for ever the interest of his people, because his interest lives beyond his life; it must live in his fame—it must live in the tenderness of his solicitude for an unborn posterity—it must live in that heart-attaching bond by which millions of men have united the destinies of themselves and their children with his, and call him by the endearing appellation of king and father of his people.

But I ask you, particularly at this momentous period, what guilt can you find? My client saw the scene of horror and blood which covers almost the face of Europe. He feared that causes which he thought similar might produce similar effects; and he sought to avert those dangers by calling the united virtue and tried moderation of the country into a state of strength and vigilance. Yet this is the conduct which the prosecution of this day seeks to stigmatize; and this is the language for which this paper is reprobated to-day as tending to turn the hearts of the people against their sovereign and inviting them to overturn the Constitution.

Let us now, gentlemen, consider the concluding part of this publication. It recommends a meeting of the people to deliberate on constitutional methods of redressing grievances. Upon this subject I am inclined to suspect that I have in my youth taken up crude ideas, not founded, perhaps in law; but I did imagine that when the Bill of Rights restored the right of petitioning for the redress of grievances it was understood that the people might boldly state among themselves that grievances did exist; that they might lawfully assemble themselves in such a manner as they might deem most orderly and decorous. I thought I had collected it from the greatest luminaries of the law. The power of petitioning seemed to me to imply the right of assembling for the purpose of deliberation. The law requiring a petition to be presented by a limited number seemed to me to admit that the petition might be prepared by any number whatever, provided, in doing so, they did not commit any breach or violation of the public peace.

It is a melancholy story that the lower orders of the people here have less means of being enlightened than the same class of people in any other country. If there be no means left by which public measures can be canvassed, what will be the consequence? Where the Press is free, and discussion unrestrained, the mind, by the collision of intercourse, gets rid of its own asperities; a sort of insensible perspiration takes place in the body politic by which those acrimonies which would otherwise fester and inflame are quietly dissolved and dissipated.

But now, if any aggregate assembly shall meet, they are censured; if a printer publishes their resolutions he is punished: rightly, to be sure, in both cases, for it has been lately done. If the people say, Let us not create tumult, but meet in delegation, they can not do it; if they are anxious to promote parliamentary reform in that way they can not do it; the law of the last session has for the first time declared such meetings to be a crime.

What then remains? The liberty of the Press only—that sacred palladium which no influence, no power, no minister, no government, which nothing but the depravity or folly or corruption of a jury can ever destroy.

And what calamities are the people saved from

by having public communication left open to them? I will tell you, gentlemen, what they are saved from, and what the government is saved from; I will tell you, also, to what both are exposed by shutting up that communication. In one case sedition speaks aloud and walks abroad; the demagog goes forth; the public eye is upon him; he frets his busy hour upon the stage; but soon either weariness, or bribe, or punishment, or disappointment bears him down or drives him off, and he appears no more.

In the other case, how does the work of sedition go forward? Night after night the muffled rebel steals forth in the dark and casts another and another brand upon the pile, to which, when the hour of fatal maturity shall arrive, he will apply the torch. If you doubt of the horrid consequence of suppressing the effusion even of individual discontent, look to those enslaved countries where the protection of despotism is supposed to be secured by such restraints. Even the person of the despot there is never in safety. Neither the fears of the despot nor the machinations of the slave have any slumber—the one anticipating the moment of peril, the other watching the opportunity of aggression.

The fatal crisis is equally a surprise upon both; the decisive instant is precipitated without warning—by folly on the one side, or by frenzy on the other; and there is no notice of the treason till the traitor acts. In those unfortunate countries—one can not read it without horror—there are officers whose province it is to have the water which is to be drunk by their rulers sealed up in bottles lest some wretched miscreant should throw poison into the draught.

But, gentlemen, if you wish for a nearer and more interesting example, you have it in the history of your own revolution. You have it at that memorable period when the monarch[1] found a servile acquiescence in the ministers of his folly—when the liberty of the Press was trodden under foot—when venal sheriffs returned packed juries, to carry into effect those fatal conspiracies of the few against the many—when the devoted benches of public justice were filled by some of those foundlings of fortune who, overwhelmed in the torrent of corruption at an early period, lay at the bottom like drowned bodies while soundness or sanity remained in them; but at length, becoming buoyant by putrifaction, they rose as they rotted, and floated to the surface of the polluted stream, where they were drifted along, the objects of terror, and contagion, and abomination.

In that awful moment of a nation's travail, of the last gasp of tyranny and the first breath of freedom, how pregnant is the example! The Press extinguished, the people enslaved, and the prince undone. As the advocate of society, therefore—of peace—of domestic liberty—and the lasting union of the two countries—I conjure you to guard the liberty of the Press, that great

---

[1] James II.

sentinel of the State, that grand detector of public imposture; guard it because, when it sinks, there sinks with it in one common grave the liberty of the subject and the security of the Crown.

Gentlemen, I am glad that this question has not been brought forward earlier; I rejoice for the sake of the court, of the jury, and of the public repose, that this question has not been brought forward till now. In Great Britain analogous circumstances have taken place. At the commencement of that unfortunate war which has deluged Europe with blood, the spirit of the English people was tremblingly alive to the terror of French principles; at that moment of general paroxysm, to accuse was to convict. The danger looked larger to the public eye from the misty region through which it was surveyed. We measure inaccessible heights by the shadows which they project, where the lowness and the distance of the light form the length of the shade.

There is a sort of aspiring and adventurous credulity which disdains assenting to obvious truths and delights in catching at the improbability of circumstances as its best ground of faith. To what other cause, gentlemen, can you ascribe that, in the wise, the reflecting, and the philosophic nation of Great Britain, a printer has been found guilty of a libel for publishing those resolutions to which the present minister of that kingdom had actually subscribed his name?

To what other cause can you ascribe, what in my mind is still more astonishing, in such a country as Scotland, a nation cast in the happy medium between the spiritless acquiescence of submissive poverty and the sturdy credulity of pampered wealth; cool and ardent, adventurous and persevering; winging her eagle flight against the blaze of every science, with an eye that never winks, and a wing that never tires; crowned as she is with the spoils of every art, and decked with the wreath of every muse; from the deep and scrutinizing researches of her Hume, to the sweet and simple, but not the less sublime and pathetic morality of her Burns [1]—how, from the bosom of a country like that, genius and character and talents should be banished to a distant, barbarous soil; condemned to pine under the horrid communion of vulgar vice and baseborn profligacy for twice the period that ordinary calculation gives to the continuance of human life?

But I will not further press any idea that is painful to me and I am sure must be painful to you. I will only say you have now an example of which neither England nor Scotland had the advantage. You have the example of the panic, the infatuation, and the contrition of both. It is now for you to decide whether you will profit by their experience of idle panic and idle regret,

[1] Hume at this time had been dead twenty years, but Burns was still living, a third edition of his poems having appeared the year before Curran's speech was made.

or whether you merely prefer to palliate a servile imitation of their frailty by a paltry affectation of their repentance. It is now for you to show that you are not carried away by the same hectic delusions to acts of which no tears can wash away the consequences or the indelible reproach.

I agree most implicitly with Mr. Attorney-General that nothing can be more criminal than an attempt to work a change in the government by armed force, and I entreat that the court will not suffer any expression of mine to be considered as giving encouragement or defense to any design to excite disaffection, to overawe or to overturn the government. But I put my client's case upon another ground. If he was led into an opinion of grievances where there were none; if he thought there ought to be a reform where none was necessary, he is answerable only for his intention. He can be answerable to you in the same way only that he is answerable to that God before whom the accuser, the accused, and the judge must appear together; that is, not for the clearness of his understanding, but for the purity of his heart.

Gentlemen, Mr. Attorney-General has said that Mr. Rowan did by this publication (supposing it to be his) recommend, under the name of equality, a general, indiscriminate assumption of public rule by every meanest person in the State. Low as we are in point of public information, there is not, I believe, any man, who thinks for a moment, that does not know that all which the great body of the people of any country can have from any government is a fair encouragement to their industry and protection for the fruits of their labor. And there is scarcely any man, I believe, who does not know that if a people could become so silly as to abandon their stations in society under pretense of governing themselves, they would become the dupes and the victims of their own folly. But does this publication recommend any such infatuated abandonment or any such desperate assumption?

Gentlemen, let me suggest another observation or two. If still you have any doubt as to the guilt or innocence of the defendant, give me leave to suggest to you what circumstances you ought to consider in order to found your verdict. You should consider the character of the person accused, and in this your task is easy. I will venture to say there is not a man in this nation more known than the gentleman who is the subject of this prosecution, not only by the part he has taken in public concerns, and which he has taken in common with many, but still more so by that extraordinary sympathy for human affliction which, I am sorry to think, he shares with so small a number.

There is not a day that you hear the cries of your starving manufacturers in your streets, that you do not also see the advocate of their sufferings; that you do not see his honest and manly figure, with uncovered head soliciting for their relief, searching the frozen heart of charity for every string that can be touched by compassion, and urging the force of every argument and every motive save that which his modesty suppresses—the authority of his own generous example. Or, if you see him not there, you may trace his steps to the private abode of disease and famine and despair; the messenger of Heaven, bearing with him food, and medicine, and consolation.

Are these the materials of which anarchy and public rapine are to be formed? Is this the man on whom to fasten the abominable charge of goading on a frantic populace to mutiny and bloodshed? Is this the man likely to apostatize from every principle that can bind him to the State, his birth, his property, his education, his character, and his children?

Let me tell you, gentlemen of the jury, if you agree with his prosecutors in thinking that there ought to be a sacrifice of such a man, on such an occasion, and upon the credit of such evidence, you are to convict him—never did you, never can you give a sentence, consigning any man to public punishment with less danger to his person or to his fame; for where could the hireling be found to fling contumely or ingratitude at his head, whose private distress he had not labored to alleviate, or whose public condition he had not labored to improve.

The man will be weighed against the charge, the witness, and the sentence; and impartial justice will demand, why has an Irish jury done this deed? The moment he ceases to be regarded as a criminal, he becomes of necessity an accuser. And, let me ask you, what can your most zealous defenders be prepared to answer to such a charge? When your sentence shall have sent him forth to that stage which guilt alone can render infamous, let me tell you he will not be like a little statue upon a mighty pedestal, diminishing by elevation, but he will stand a striking and imposing object upon a monument which, if it does not, and it can not, record the atrocity of his crime, must record the atrocity of his conviction. And upon this subject credit me when I say that I am still more anxious for you than I can possibly be for him. I can not but feel the peculiarity of your situation—not the jury of his own choice, which the law of England allows, but which ours refuses, collected in that box by a person certainly no friend to Mr. Rowan, certainly not very deeply interested in giving him a very impartial jury.

Feeling this, as I am persuaded you do, you can not be surprised, however you may be distressed, at the mournful presage with which an anxious public is led to fear the worst from your possible determination. But I will not, for the justice and honor of our common country, suffer my mind to be borne away by such melancholy anticipations. I will not relinquish the confidence that this day will be the period of his sufferings; and, however mercilessly he has been hitherto pursued, that your verdict will send him home to the arms of his family and the wishes of his country. But if—which Heaven forbid—it has still been unfortunately determined that, because he has not bent to power and authority, because he would not bow down before the golden calf and worship it, he is to be bound and cast into the furnace, I do trust in God that there is a redeeming spirit in the Constitution which will be seen to walk with the sufferer through the flames and to preserve him unhurt by the conflagration.

II

AT THE PROSECUTION OF JOHNSON FOR LIBEL[1]

(1805)

I NOW address you on a question the most vitally connected with the liberty and well-being of every man within the limits of the British Empire—which being decided one way, he may be a freeman; which being decided the other, he must be a slave. I refer to the maintenance of that sacred security for the freedom of English-

---

[1] From a speech in the Court of Exchequer in the case of the king against Mr. Justice Johnson, on February 4, 1805. At the conclusion of this speech one of the judges, Lord Avonmore, could not restrain his tears. After the court adjourned he sent for Curran and as Curran entered his private room embraced him. This proved to be the beginning of a reconciliation after what had been a serious breach between these men.

men—so justly called the second Magna Charta
of British liberty—the Habeas Corpus Act: the
spirit and letter of which is, that the party arrested shall without a moment's delay be bailed,
if the offense be bailable. What was the occasion
of the law? The arbitrary transportation of the
subject beyond the realm; the base and malignant war which the odious and despicable minions of power are for ever ready to wage against
all those who are honest and bold enough to
despise, to expose, and to resist them.

Such is the oscitancy of man, that he lies tor-
pid for ages under these aggressions, until, at
last, some signal abuse—the violation of Lucrece,
the death of Virginia, the oppression of William
Tell—shakes him from his slumber. For years
had those drunken gambols of power been played
in England; for years had the waters of bitter-
ness been rising to the brim; at last, a single
drop caused them to overflow—the oppression of
a single individual raised the people of England
from their sleep. And what does that great
Statute do? It defines and asserts the right, it
points out the abuse; and it endeavors to secure
the right, and to guard against the abuse, by
giving redress to the sufferer, and by punishing
the offender. For years had it been the practise
to transport obnoxious persons out of the realm
into distant parts, under the pretext of punishment, or of safe custody. Well might they have
been said, to be sent "to that undiscovered country from whose bourn no traveler returns"; for

of these wretched travelers how few ever did return!

But of that flagrant abuse this Statute has laid the ax to the root. It prohibits the abuse; it declares such detention or removal illegal; it gives an action against all persons concerned in the offense, by contriving, writing, signing, countersigning such warrant, or advising or assisting therein. Are bulwarks like these ever constructed to repel the incursions of a contemptible enemy? Was it a trivial and ordinary occasion which raised this storm of indignation in the Parliament of that day? Is the ocean ever lashed by the tempest, to waft a feather, or to drown a fly? By this Act you have a solemn legislative declaration, "that it is incompatible with liberty to send any subject out of the realm, under pretense of any crime supposed or alleged to be committed in a foreign jurisdiction, except that crime be capital." Such were the bulwarks which our ancestors placed about the sacred temple of liberty, such the ramparts by which they sought to bar out the ever-toiling ocean of arbitrary power; and thought (generous credulity!) that they had barred it out from their posterity forever. Little did they foresee the future race of vermin that would work their way through those mounds, and let back the inundation!

I am not ignorant, my lord, that the extraordinary construction of law against which I contend has received the sanction of another court, nor of the surprise and dismay with which it smote upon the general heart of the bar. I am aware that I may have the mortification of being told, in another country, of that unhappy decision; and I foresee in what confusion I shall hang down my head when I am told it.

But I cherish, too, the consolatory hope, that I shall be able to tell them that I had an old and learned friend, whom I would put above all the sweepings of their hall; who was of a different opinion; who had derived his ideas of civil liberty from the purest fountains of Athens and of Rome; who had fed the youthful vigor of his studious mind with the theoretic knowledge of their wisest philosophers and statesmen, and who had refined that theory into the quick and exquisite sensibility of moral instinct, by contemplating the practise of their most illustrious examples, by dwelling on the sweet-souled piety of Simon, on the anticipated Christianity of Socrates, on the gallant and pathetic patriotism of Epaminondas, on that pure austerity of Fabricius, whom to move from his integrity would have been more difficult than to have pushed the sun from his course.

I would add that, if he had seemed to hesitate, it was but for a moment; that his hesitation was like the passing cloud that floats across the morning sun, and hides it from the view, and does so for a moment hide it, by involving the spectator, without even approaching the face of the luminary. And this soothing hope I draw from the dearest and tenderest recollections of my life; from the remembrance of those attic nights and those refections of the gods which we have partaken with those admired, and respected, and beloved companions, who have gone before us,—over whose ashes the most precious tears of Ireland have been shed.

Yes, my good lord, I see you do not forget them; I see their sacred forms passing in sad review before your memory; I see your pained and softened fancy recalling those happy meetings, where the innocent enjoyment of social mirth became expanded into the nobler warmth of social virtue, and the horizon of the board became enlarged into the horizon of man; where the swelling heart conceived and communicated the pure and generous purpose; where my slenderer and younger taper inbibed its borrowed light from the more matured and redundant fountain of yours. Yes, my lord, we can remember those nights, without any other regret than that they can never more return; for,

> "We spent them not in toys, or lust, or wine;
>   But search of deep philosophy,
>   Wit, eloquence, and poesy;
> Arts which I loved, for they, my friends, were
>   thine."

WOLF TONE

ON BEING FOUND GUILTY [1]

(1798)

Born in 1763, died in 1798; promoted and served in the Expedition of Hoche to Ireland in 1796; captured on a French squadron bound for Ireland in 1798; on being sentenced to death, he committed suicide.

I MEAN not to give you the trouble of bringing judicial proof to convict me legally of having acted in hostility to the government of his Britannic majesty in Ireland. I admit the fact. From my earliest youth I have regarded the connection between Great Britain and Ireland as the curse of the Irish nation, and felt convinced that, while it lasted, this country could never be free nor happy. My mind has been confirmed in this opinion by the experience

---

[1] Addressed to the court-martial assembled to try him in the Dublin barracks in November, 1798. Tone is described as having been "dressed in the French uniform; a large cocked hat with broad gold lace and the tri-colored cockade; a blue uniform coat with gold-embroidered collar and two large gold epaulettes; blue pantaloons with gold lace garters at the knee, and short boots bound at the top with gold lace." He was found guilty and sentenced to death on his own confession. His request that he might be shot, instead of hanged, and thus die a soldier's death, was refused. While awaiting execution he committed suicide in order to escape the gallows.

The Irish revolt had begun in the year of Tone's arrest and conviction—1798. It was suppressed about a year later after many thousands of lives had been lost on each side.

of every succeeding year, and the conclusions which I have drawn from every fact before my eyes. In consequence, I was determined to employ all the powers which my individual efforts could move, in order to separate the two countries. That Ireland was not able of herself to throw off the yoke, I knew; I therefore sought for aid wherever it was to be found. In honorable poverty I rejected offers which, to a man in my circumstances, might be considered highly advantageous. I remained faithful to what I thought the cause of my country, and sought in the French Republic an ally to rescue three millions of my countrymen.

Attached to no party in the French Republic —without interest, without money, without intrigue— the openness and integrity of my views raised me to a high and confidential rank in its armies. I obtained the confidence of the executive directory, the approbation of my generals, and I will venture to add, the esteem and affection of my brave comrades. When I review these circumstances, I feel a secret and internal consolation, which no reverse of fortune, no sentence in the power of this court to inflict, can deprive me of, or weaken in any degree. Under the flag of the French Republic I originally engaged with a view to save and liberate my own country. For that purpose I have encountered the chances of war among strangers; for that purpose I repeatedly braved the terrors of the ocean, covered, as I knew it to be, with the triumphant fleets of that power which it was my glory and my duty to oppose. I have sacrificed all my views in life; I have courted poverty; I have left a beloved wife unprotected, and children whom I adored fatherless.

After such a sacrifice, in a cause which I have always considered—conscientiously considered—as the cause of justice and freedom, it is no great effort, at this day, to add the sacrifice of my life.

But I hear it is said that this unfortunate country has been a prey to all sorts of horrors. I sincerely lament it. I beg, however, that it may be remembered that I have been absent four years from Ireland. To me those sufferings can never be attributed. I designed by fair and open war to procure a separation of two countries. For open war I was prepared, but instead of that a system of private assassination has taken place. I repeat, while I deplore it, that it is not chargeable on me. Atrocities, it seems, have been committed on both sides. I do not less deplore them. I detest them from my heart; and to those who know my character and sentiments, I may safely appeal for the truth of this assertion: with them I need no justification. In a case like this success is everything. Success, in the eyes of the vulgar, fixes its merits. Washington succeeded, and Kosciusko failed.

After a combat nobly sustained—a combat which would have excited the respect and sympathy of a generous enemy—my fate has been to become a prisoner, to the eternal disgrace of those who gave the orders. I was brought here in irons like a felon. I mention this for the sake of others; for me, I am indifferent to it. I am aware of the fate which awaits me, and scorn equally the tone of complaint, and that of supplication. As to the connection between this country and Great Britain, I repeat it—all that has been imputed to me (words, writings, and actions), I here deliberately avow. I have spoken and acted with reflection, and on principle, and am ready to meet the consequences. Whatever be the sentence of the court, I am prepared for it. Its members will surely discharge their duty —I shall take care not to be wanting in mine.

I wish to offer a few words relative to one single point—the mode of punishment. In France our *emigrees*, who stand nearly in the same situation in which I now stand before you, are condemned to be shot. I ask that the court adjudge me the death of a soldier, and let me be shot by a platoon of grenadiers. I request this indulgence rather in consideration of the uniform I wear—the uniform of a *chef de bridage* in the French army—than from any personal regard to myself. In order to evince my claim to this favor, I beg that the court may take the trouble to peruse my commission and letters of service in the French army. It will appear from these papers that I have not received them as a mask to cover me, but that I have been long and *bona fide* an officer in the French service.

I have labored to create a people in Ireland by raising three millions of my countrymen to the rank of citizens. I have labored to abolish the infernal spirit of religious persecution, by uniting the Catholics and Dissenters. To the former I owe more than ever can be repaid. The services I was so fortunate as to render them they rewarded munificently; but they did more: when the public cry was raised against me— when the friends of my youth swarmed off and let me alone—the Catholics did not desert me; they had the virtue even to sacrifice their own interests to a rigid principle of honor; they refused, tho strongly urged, to disgrace a man who, whatever his conduct toward the government might have been, had faithfully and conscientiously discharged his duty toward them; and in so doing, tho it was in my own case, I will say they showed an instance of public virtue of which I know not whether there exists another example.[1]

---

[1] This paragraph in Tone's speech was long suppressed, being first published in 1859, with the "correspondence" of Cornwallis, the lord-lieutenant of Ireland of 1790.

EMMET

ON BEING FOUND GUILTY OF TREASON[1]
(1803)

Born in 1778, died in 1803; became a leader of the United Irishmen, and in 1803 led an unsuccessful rising in Dublin; escaping to the mountains he returned to Dublin to take leave of his fiancée, Sarah Curran, daughter of the orator, and was captured and hanged.

MY LORDS: —What have I to say why sentence of death should not be pronounced on me according to law? I have nothing to say that can alter your predetermination, nor that it will become me to say with any view to the mitigation of that sentence which you are here to pronounce, and I must abide by. But I have that to say which interests me more than life, and which you have labored (as was necessarily your office in the present circumstances of this

[1] Delivered at the Session House in Dublin before the court which had convicted him of high treason, September 19, 1803. Emmet, at that time only twenty-three years old, had taken part in a rebellion against the government. The famous address here given was an impromptu one, delivered while Emmet stood forward in the dock in front of the bench. Curran's daughter, to whom Emmet was engaged, and of whom Moore wrote the poem beginning, "She is far from the land where her young hero sleeps," two years afterward married an officer of some distinction in the Royal Staff Corps, Major Sturgeon. She died in Sicily a few months later—it is said of a broken heart.

oppressed country) to destroy. I have much to say why my reputation should be rescued from the load of false accusation and calumny which has been heaped upon it. I do not imagine that, seated where you are, your minds can be so free from impurity as to receive the least impression from what I am going to utter—I have no hopes that I can anchor my character in the breast of a court constituted and trammeled as this is— I only wish, and it is the utmost I expect, that your lordships may suffer it to float down your memories untainted by the foul breath of prejudice, until it finds some more hospitable harbor to shelter it from the storm by which it is at present buffeted.

Was I only to suffer death after being adjudged guilty by *your* tribunal, I should bow in silence, and meet the fate that awaits me without a murmur; but the sentence of law which delivers my body to the executioner, will, through the ministry of that law, labor in its own vindication to consign my character to obloquy—for there must be guilt somewhere: whether in the sentence of the court or in the catastrophe, posterity must determine. A man in my situation, my lords, has not only to encounter the difficulties of fortune, and the force of power over minds which it has corrupted or subjugated, but the difficulties of established prejudice: the man dies, but his memory lives. That mine may not perish, that it may live in the respect of my countrymen, I seize upon this opportunity to vindicate myself from some of the charges alleged against me. When my spirit shall be wafted to a more friendly port; when my shade shall have joined the bands of those martyred heroes who have shed their blood on the scaffold and in the field, in defense of their country and of virtue, this is my hope: I wish that my memory and name may animate those who survive me, while I look down with complacency on the destruction of that perfidious government which upholds its domination by blasphemy of the Most High— which displays its power over man as over the beasts of the forest—which sets man upon his brother, and lifts his hand in the name of God against the throat of his fellow who believes or doubts a little more or a little less than the government standard—a government which is steeled to barbarity by the cries of the orphans and the tears of the widows which it has made.[1]

I appeal to the immaculate God—I swear by the throne of Heaven, before which I must shortly appear—by the blood of the murdered patriots who have gone before me—that my conduct has been through all this peril and all my purposes, governed only by the convictions which I have uttered, and by no other view, than that of their cure, and the emancipation of my country from the superinhuman oppression under which she has so long and too patiently travailed;

[1] At this period Lord Norbury interrupted Emmet, saying severely, that the mean and wicked enthusiasts who felt as he did "were not equal to the accomplishment of their wild designs."

and that I confidently and assuredly hope that, wild and chimerical as it may appear, there is still union and strength in Ireland to accomplish this noble enterprise. Of this I speak with the confidence of intimate knowledge, and with the consolation that appertains to that confidence. Think not, my lords, I say this for the petty gratification of giving you a transitory uneasiness; a man who never yet raised his voice to assert a lie, will not hazard his character with posterity by asserting a falsehood on a subject so important to his country, and on an occasion like this. Yes, my lords, a man who does not wish to have his epitaph written until his country is liberated, will not leave a weapon in the power of envy; nor a pretense to impeach the probity which he means to preserve even in the grave to which tyranny consigns him.[1]

Again I say, that what I have spoken, was not intended for your lordship, whose situation I commiserate rather than envy—my expressions were for my countrymen; if there is a true Irishman present, let my last words cheer him in the hour of his affliction.[2]

I have always understood it to be the duty of a judge when a prisoner has been convicted, to pronounce the sentence of the law; I have also understood that judges sometimes think it their duty to hear with patience, and to speak with

[1] Here he was again interrupted by the court.

[2] Again Emmet was interrupted, Lord Norbury saying he did not sit there to hear treason.

humanity; to exhort the victim of the laws, and to offer with tender benignity his opinions of the motives by which he was actuated in the crime, of which he had been adjudged guilty: that a judge has thought it his duty so to have done, I have no doubt—but where is the boasted freedom of your institutions, where is the vaunted impartiality, clemency, and mildness of your courts of justice, if an unfortunate prisoner, whom your policy, and not pure justice, is about to deliver into the hands of the executioner, is not suffered to explain his motives sincerely and truly, and to vindicate the principles by which he was actuated?

My lords, it may be a part of the system of angry justice, to bow a man's mind by humiliation to the purposed ignominy of the scaffold; but worse to me than the purposed shame, or the scaffold's terrors, would be the shame of such unfounded imputations as have been laid against me in this court: you, my lord [Lord Norbury], are a judge, I am the supposed culprit; I am a man, you are a man also; by a revolution of power, we might change places, tho we never could change characters; if I stand at the bar of this court, and dare not vindicate my character, what a farce is your justice? If I stand at this bar and dare not vindicate my character, how dare you calumniate it? Does the sentence of death which your unhallowed policy inflicts on my body, also condemn my tongue to silence and my reputation to reproach? Your executioner

may abridge the period of my existence, but while
I exist I shall not forbear to vindicate my character and motives from your aspersions; and as
a man to whom fame is dearer than life, I will
make the last use of that life in doing justice to
that reputation which is to live after me, and
which is the only legacy I can leave to those I
honor and love, and for whom I am proud to
perish. As men, my lord, we must appear at the
great day at one common tribunal, and it will
then remain for the searcher of all hearts to
show a collective universe who was engaged in
the most virtuous actions, or actuated by the
purest motives—my country's oppressors or——[1]

My lord, will a dying man be denied the legal
privilege of exculpating himself, in the eyes of
the community, of an undeserved reproach
thrown upon him during his trial, by charging
him with ambition, and attempting to cast away,
for a paltry consideration, the liberties of his
country? Why did your lordship insult me? or
rather why insult justice, in demanding of me
why sentence of death should not be pronounced?
I know, my lord, that form prescribes that you
should ask the question; the form also presumes
a right of answering. This no doubt may be
dispensed with—and so might the whole cere-
mony of trial, since sentence was already pronounced at the castle, before your jury was im-
paneled; your lordships are but the priests of

---

[1] Here Emmet was told to listen to the sentence of the law.

the oracle, and I submit; but I insist on the whole of the forms.

I am charged with being an emissary of France! An emissary of France! And for what end? It is alleged that I wished to sell the independence of my country! And for what end? Was this the object of my ambition? And is this the mode by which a tribunal of justice reconciles contradictions? No, I am no emissary; and my ambition was to hold a place among the deliverers of my country—not in power, nor in profit, but in the glory of the achievement! Sell my country's independence to France! And for what? Was it for a change of masters? No! But for ambition! O my country, was it personal ambition that could influence me? Had it been the soul of my actions, could I not by my education and fortune, by the rank and consideration of my family, have placed myself among the proudest of my oppressors? My country was my idol; to it I sacrificed every selfish, every endearing sentiment; and for it, I now offer up my life. O God! No, my lord; I acted as an Irishman, determined on delivering my country from the yoke of a foreign and unrelenting tyranny, and from the more galling yoke of a domestic faction, which is its joint partner and perpetrator in the parricide, for the ignominy of existing with an exterior of splendor and of conscious depravity. It was the wish of my heart to extricate my country from this doubly riveted despotism.

I wished to place her independence beyond the reach of any power on earth; I wished to exalt you to that proud station in the world.

Connection with France was indeed intended, but only as far as mutual interest would sanction or require. Were they to assume any authority inconsistent with the purest independence, it would be the signal for their destruction; we sought aid, and we sought it, as we had assurances we should obtain it—as auxiliaries in war and allies in peace.

Were the French to come as invaders or enemies, uninvited by the wishes of the people, I should oppose them to the utmost of my strength. Yes, my countrymen, I should advise you to meet them on the beach, with a sword in one hand, and a torch in the other; I would meet them with all the destructive fury of war; and I would animate my countrymen to immolate them in their boats, before they had contaminated the soil of my country. If they succeeded in landing, and if forced to retire before superior discipline, I would dispute every inch of ground, burn every blade of grass, and the last intrenchment of liberty should be my grave. What I could not do myself, if I should fall, I should leave as a last charge to my countrymen to accomplish; because I should feel conscious that life, any more than death, is unprofitable, when a foreign nation holds my country in subjection.

But it was not as an enemy that the succors of France were to land. I looked indeed for the assistance of France; but I wished to prove to France and to the world that Irishmen deserved to be assisted!—that they were indignant at slavery, and ready to assert the independence and liberty of their country.

I wished to procure for my country the guarantee which Washington procured for America. To procure an aid, which, by its example, would be as important as its valor, disciplined, gallant, pregnant with science and experience; which would perceive the good, and polish the rough points of our character. They would come to us as strangers, and leave us as friends, after sharing in our perils and elevating our destiny. These were my objects—not to receive new taskmasters, but to expel old tyrants; these were my views, and these only became Irishmen. It was for these ends I sought aid from France; because France, even as an enemy, could not be more implacable than the enemy already in the bosom of my country.[1]

I have been charged with that importance in the efforts to emancipate my country, as to be considered the *keystone* of the combination of Irishmen; or, as your lordship expressed it, "the life and blood of conspiracy." You do me honor overmuch. You have given to the subaltern all the credit of a superior. There are men engaged in this *conspiracy*, who are not only superior to me, but even to your own conceptions

[1] Here Emmet was interrupted by the court.

of yourself, my lord; men, before the splendor of whose genius and virtues, I should bow with respectful deference, and who would think themselves dishonored to be called your friend— who would not disgrace themselves by shaking your bloodstained hand——[1]

What, my lord, shall you tell me, on the passage to that scaffold, which that tyranny, of which you are only the intermediary executioner, has erected for my murder, that I am accountable for all the blood that has and will be shed in this struggle of the oppressed against the oppressor?—shall you tell me this—and must I be so very a slave as not to repel it?

I do not fear to approach the omnipotent Judge, to answer for the conduct of my whole life; and am I to be appalled and falsified by a mere remnant of mortality here? By you, too, who, if it were possible to collect all the innocent blood that you have shed in your unhallowed ministry, in one great reservoir, your lordship might swim in it.[1]

Let no man dare, when I am dead, to charge me with dishonor; let no man attaint my memory by believing that I could have engaged in any cause but that of my country's liberty and independence; or that I could have become the pliant minion of power in the oppression or the miseries of my countrymen. The proclamation of the provisional government speaks for our

---

[1] Here Emmet was interrupted once more.
[2] Here the judge interfered.

views; no inference can be tortured from it to countenance barbarity or debasement at home, or subjection, humiliation, or treachery from abroad; I would not have submitted to a foreign oppressor for the same reason that I would resist the foreign and domestic oppressor; in the dignity of freedom I would have fought upon the threshold of my country, and its enemy should enter only by passing over my lifeless corpse. Am I, who lived but for my country, and who have subjected myself to the dangers of the jealous and watchful oppressor, and the bondage of the grave, only to give my countrymen their rights, and my country her independence, and am I to be loaded with calumny, and not suffered to resent or repel it—no, God forbid!

If the spirits of the illustrious dead participate in the concerns and cares of those who are dear to them in this transitory life—oh, ever dear and venerated shade of my departed father, look down with scrutiny upon the conduct of your suffering son; and see if I have even for a moment deviated from those principles of morality and patriotism which it was your care to instil into my youthful mind, and for which I am now to offer up my life!

My lords, you are impatient for the sacrifice— the blood which you seek is not congealed by the artificial terrors which surround your victim; it circulates warmly and unruffled, through the channels which God created for noble purposes, but which you are bent to destroy, for purposes so grievous, that they cry to heaven. Be yet patient! I have but a few words more to say. I am going to my cold and silent grave: my lamp of life is nearly extinguished: my race is run: the grave opens to receive me, and I sink into its bosom! I have but one request to ask at my departure from this world—it is the charity of its silence! Let no man write my epitaph: for as no man who knows my motives dare now vindicate them, let not prejudice or ignorance asperse them. Let them and me repose in obscurity and peace, and my tomb remain uninscribed, until other times, and other men, can do justice to my character; when my country takes her place among the nations of the earth, then, and not till then, let my epitaph be written. I have done.[1]

[1] At his execution Emmet, in passing out of his cell, met the turnkey who had been kind to him. Fettered as he was he could not shake hands with him, but instead kissed him on the cheek. The turnkey is said to have fainted then and there and not to have recovered until after Emmet was hanged and his head severed from his body.

CHARLES PHILLIPS

I

AN ADDRESS TO CATHOLICS [1]

Born about 1789, died in 1859; called to the Irish Bar in 1812; active in behalf of Catholic emancipation; called to the English Bar in 1821, and became a leader at the Old Bailey.

IT is with no small degree of self-congratulation that I at length find myself in a province which every glance of the eye and every throb of the heart tell me is truly Irish; and that congratulation is not a little enhanced by finding that you receive me not quite as a stranger.

Tho we never met, you hail in me the sweet association, and I feel myself among you even as if I were in the home of my nativity. But this my knowledge of you was not left to chance; nor was it left to the records of your charity, the memorials of your patriotism, your municipal magnificence, or your commercial splendor; it came to me hallowed by the accents of that tongue on which Ireland has so often hung with ecstasy, heightened by the eloquence

[1] Phillips, tho a Protestant, was presented with a national testimonial in recognition of his services to the cause of Catholic emancipation, as promoted by the Roman Catholic Association. The speech here given was delivered in Cork at a meeting of Roman Catholics.

and endeared by the sincerity of, I hope, our mutual friend. Let me congratulate him on having become in some degree naturalized in a province where the spirit of the elder day seems to have lingered; and let me congratulate you on the acquisition of a man who is at once the zealous advocate of your cause and a practical instance of the injustice of your oppressions. Surely, surely if merit had fair play, if splendid talents, if indefatigable industry, if great research, if unsullied principle, if a heart full of the finest affections, if a mind matured in every manly accomplishment—in short, if every noble public quality, mellowed and reflected in the pure mirror of domestic virtue, could entitle a subject to distinction in a state, Mr. O'Connell should be distinguished; but it is his crime to be a Catholic and his curse to be an Irishman.

Simpleton! he prefers his conscience to a place, and the love of his country to a participation in her plunder! Indeed, he will never rise. If he joined the bigots of my sect he might be a sergeant; if he joined the infidels of your sect he might enjoy a pension, and there is no knowing whether some Orange corporator, at an Orange anniversary, might not modestly yield him the precedence of giving "the glorious and immortal memory."

But let us turn to the contemplation of your cause, which, as far as argument can effect it, stands on a sublime and splendid elevation. Every obstacle has vanished into air; every favorable circumstance has hardened into adamant.

The pope, whom childhood was taught to lisp as the enemy of religion, and age shuddered at as a prescriptive calamity, has by his example put the princes of Christendom to shame. This day of miracles, in which the human heart has been strung to its extremest point of energy; this day, to which posterity will look for instances of every crime and every virtue, holds not in its page of wonders a more sublime phenomenon than that calumniated pontiff. Placed at the very pinnacle of human elevation, surrounded by the pomp of the Vatican and the splendors of the court, pouring the mandates of Christ from the throne of the Cæsars, nations were his subjects, kings were his companions, religion was his handmaid; he went forth gorgeous with the accumulated dignity of ages, every knee bending and every eye blessing the prince of one world and the prophet of another. Have we not seen him in one moment, his crown crumbled, his scepter a reed, his throne a shadow, his home a dungeon?

But if we have, Catholics, it was only to show how inestimable is human virtue compared with human grandeur; it was only to show those whose faith was failing and whose fears were strengthening that the simplicity of the patriarchs, the piety of the saints, and the patience of the martyrs had not wholly vanished.

Perhaps it was also ordained to show the bigot at home, as well as the tyrant abroad, that tho the person might be chained, and the motive calumniated, religion was still strong enough to support her sons and to confound if she could not reclaim her enemies. No threats could awe, no promises could tempt, no sufferings could appal him; amid the damps of his dungeon he dashed away the cup in which the pearl of his liberty was to be dissolved.

Only reflect on the state of the world at that moment. All around him was convulsed, the very foundations of the earth seemed giving way; the comet was let loose, that "from its fiery hair shook pestilence and death"; the twilight was gathering, the tempest was roaring, the darkness was at hand; but he towered sublime, like the last mountain in the deluge, majestic, not less in his elevation than in his solitude, immutable amid change, magnificent amid ruin, the last remnant of earth's beauty, the last resting-place of Heaven's light! Thus have the terrors of the Vatican retreated; thus has that cloud which hovered o'er your cause brightened at once into a sign of your faith and an assurance of your victory.

Another obstacle, the omnipotence of France; I know it was a pretense, but it was made an obstacle. What has become of it? The spell of her invincibility destroyed, the spirit of her armies broken, her immense boundary dismembered, and the lord of her empire become the exile of a rock. She allows fancy no fear, and bigotry no speciousness; and, as if in the very operation of the change to point the purpose of your redemption, the hand that replanted the rejected lily was that of an Irish Catholic.

Perhaps it is not also unworthy of remark that the last day of her triumph and the first of her decline was that on which her insatiable chieftain smote the holy head of your religion. You will hardly suspect I am imbued with the follies of superstition; but when the man now unborn shall trace the story of that eventful day he will see the adopted child of fortune borne on the wings of victory from clime to clime, marking every movement with a triumph and every pause with a crown, till time, space, and seasons, nay, even Nature herself, seeming to vanish from before him—in the blasphemy of his ambition he smote the apostle of his God and dared to raise the everlasting Cross amid his perishable trophies!

Another obstacle, the tenets of your creed. Has England still to learn them? I will tell her where. Let her ask Canada, the last plank of her American shipwreck. Let her ask Portugal, the first omen of her European splendor. Let her ask Spain, the most Catholic country in the universe, her Catholic friends, her Catholic allies, her rivals in the triumph, her reliance in the retreat, her last stay when the world had deserted her. They must have told her on the field of blood whether it was true that they "kept no faith with heretics."

Alas, alas! how miserable a thing is bigotry,

when every friend puts it to blush and every
triumph but rebukes its weakness! If England
continued still to accredit this calumny, I would
direct her for conviction to the hero, for whose
gift alone she owes us an eternity of gratitude;
whom we have seen leading the van of universal
emancipation, decking his wreath with the flowers of every soil and filling his army with the
soldiers of every sect; before whose splendid
dawn, every tear exhaling and every vapor van-
ishing, the colors of the European world have
revived and the spirit of European liberty (may
no crime avert the omen!) seems to have risen!
Suppose he was a Catholic, could this have been?
Suppose Catholics did not follow him, could this
have been? Did the Catholic Cortes inquire his
faith when they gave him the supreme command?
Did the regent of Portugal withhold from his
creed the reward of his valor? Did the Catholic
soldier pause at Salamanca to dispute upon po-
lemics? Did the Catholic chieftain prove upon
Barossa that he had kept no faith with heretics?
or did the creed of Spain, the same with that of
France, the opposite of that of England, prevent their association in the field of liberty?

Oh, no, no, no! the citizen of every clime, the
friend of every color, and the child of every
creed, Liberty walks abroad in the ubiquity of her
benevolence, alike to her the varieties of faith
and the vicissitudes of country; she has no object
but the happiness of man, no bounds but the extremities of creation. Yes, yes, it was reserved

for Wellington to redeem his own country when he was regenerating every other. It was reserved for him to show how vile were the aspersions on your creed, how generous were the glowings of your gratitude.

He was a Protestant, yet Catholics trusted him; he was a Protestant, yet Catholics advanced him. He is a Protestant Knight in Catholic Portugal; he is a Protestant Duke in Catholic Spain; he is a Protestant commander of Catholic armies. He is more: he is the living proof of the Catholic's liberality and the undeniable refutation of the Protestant's injustice. Gentlemen, as a Protestant, tho I may blush for the bigotry of many of my creed who continue obstinate, in the teeth of this conviction, still, were I a Catholic, I should feel little triumph in the victory. I should only hang my head at the distresses which this warfare occasioned to my country. I should only think how long she had withered in the agony of her disunion; how long she had bent, fettered by slaves, cajoled by blockheads and plundered by adventurers; the proverb of the fool, the prey of the politician, the dupe of the designing, the experiment of the desperate; struggling as it were between her own fanatical and infatuated parties, those hell-engendered serpents which enfold her, like the Trojan seer, even at the worship of her altars, and crush her to death in the very embraces of her children! It is time (is it not?) that she should be extricated.

But to what end do I argue with the bigot?—a wretch whom no philosophy can humanize, no charity soften, no religion reclaim, no miracle convert; a monster who, red with the fires of hell and bending under the crimes of earth, erects his murderous divinity upon a throne of skulls, and would gladly feed, even with a brother's blood, the cannibal appetite of his rejected altar! His very interest can not soften him into humanity. Surely if it could, no man would be found mad enough to advocate a system which cankers the very heart of society and undermines the natural resources of government; which takes away the strongest excitement to industry by closing up every avenue to laudable ambition; which administers to the vanity or the vice of a party when it should only study the advantage of a people; and holds out the perquisites of state as an impious bounty on the persecution of religion.

My friends, farewell! This has been a most unexpected meeting to me; it has been our first—it may be our last. I can never forget the enthusiasm of this reception. I am too much affected by it to make professions; but, believe me, no matter where I may be driven by the whim of my destiny, you shall find me one in whom change of place shall create no change of principle, one whose memory must perish ere he forgets his country, whose heart must be cold when it beats not for her happiness.

II

THE CHARACTER OF NAPOLEON[1]
(About 1817)

HE is fallen! We may now pause before that splendid prodigy, which towered among us like some ancient ruin, whose frown terrified the glance its magnificence attracted.

Grand, gloomy, and peculiar, he sat upon the throne, a sceptered hermit, wrapped in the solitude of his own originality.

A mind bold, independent, and decisive—a will, despotic in its dictates—an energy that distanced expedition, and a conscience pliable to every touch of interest, marked the outline of this extraordinary character—the most extraordinary, perhaps, that, in the annals of this world, ever rose, or reigned, or fell.

Flung into life, in the midst of a revolution that quickened every energy of a people who acknowledged no superior, he commenced his course, a stranger by birth, and a scholar by charity!

With no friend but his sword, and no fortune but his talents, he rushed into the lists where rank, and wealth, and genius had arrayed them-

[1] This specimen of Phillips' style is probably the most successful of his grandiloquent efforts. It has long been familiar in the mouths of schoolboys. Its date is about the year of the second Restoration, after the exile of Napoleon to St. Helena.

selves, and competition fled from him as from the glance of destiny. He knew no motive but interest—he acknowledged no criterion but success—he worshiped no God but ambition, and with an Eastern devotion he knelt at the shrine of his idolatry. Subsidiary to this, there was no creed that he did not profess, there was no opinion that he did not promulgate: in the hope of a dynasty, he upheld the crescent; for the sake of a divorce, he bowed before the Cross: the orphan of St. Louis, he became the adopted child of the Republic; and with a paricidal ingratitude, on the ruins both of the throne and the tribune, he reared the throne of his despotism.

A professed Catholic, he imprisoned the pope; a pretended patriot, he impoverished the country; and in the name of Brutus, he grasped without remorse, and wore without shame, the diadem of the Cæsars!

Through this pantomime of his policy, fortune played the clown to his caprices. At his touch, crowns crumbled, beggars reigned, systems vanished, the wildest theories took the color of his whim, and all that was venerable, and all that was novel, changed places with the rapidity of a drama. Even apparent defeat assumed the appearance of victory—his flight from Egypt confirmed his destiny—ruin itself only elevated him to empire.

But if his fortune was great, his genius was transcendent; decision flashed upon his counsels; and it was the same to decide and to perform.

To inferior intellects, his combinations appeared perfectly impossible, his plans perfectly impracticable; but, in his hands, simplicity marked their development, and success vindicated their adoption.

His person partook the character of his mind—if the one never yielded in the cabinet, the other never bent in the field.

Nature had no obstacles that he did not surmount—space no opposition that he did not spurn; and whether amid Alpine rocks, Arabian sands, or polar snows, he seemed proof against peril, and empowered with ubiquity! The whole continent of Europe trembled at beholding the audacity of his designs, and the miracle of their execution. Skepticism bowed to the prodigies of his performance; romance assumed the air of history; nor was there aught too incredible for belief, or too fanciful for expectation, when the world saw a subaltern of Corsica waving his imperial flag over her most ancient capitals. All the visions of antiquity became common places in his contemplation; kings were his people—nations were his outposts; and he disposed of courts, and crowns, and camps, and churches, and cabinets, as if they were the titular dignitaries of the chess-board!

Amid all these changes he stood immutable as adamant. It mattered little whether in the field or the drawing-room—with the mob or the levee—wearing the jacobin bonnet or the iron crown—banishing a Braganza, or espousing a Haps-

burg—dictating peace on a raft to the Czar of
Russia, or contemplating defeat at the gallows of
Leipsic—he was still the same military despot!

Cradled in the camp, he was to the last hour
the darling of the army; and whether in the
camp or the cabinet, he never forsook a friend or
forgot a favor. Of all his soldiers, not one
abandoned him, till affection was useless; and
their first stipulation was for the safety of their
favorite.

They knew well that if he was lavish of them,
he was prodigal of himself; and that if he exposed them to peril, he repaid them with plunder. For the soldier, he subsidized every people;
to the people he made even pride pay tribute.
The victorious veteran glittered with his gains;
and the capital, gorgeous with the spoils of art,
became the miniature metropolis of the universe.
In this wonderful combination, his affectation of
literature must not be omitted. The jailer of
the Press, he affected the patronage of letters—
the proscriber of books, he encouraged philosophy—the persecutor of authors, and the mur-
derer of printers, he yet pretended to the protection of learning!—the assassin of Palm, the
silencer of De Stael, and the denouncer of Kotze-
bue, he was the friend of David, the benefactor
of De Lille, and sent his academic prize to the
philosopher of England.

Such a medley of contradictions, and at the
same time such an individual consistency, were
never united in the same character. A Royalist

—a Republican and an Emperor—a Mohammedan—a Catholic and a Patron of the Synagog—a Subaltern and a Sovereign—a Traitor and a Tyrant—a Christian and an Infidel—he was, through all his vicissitudes, the same stern, impatient, inflexible original—the same mysterious incomprehensible self—the man without a model, and without a shadow.

His fall, like his life, baffled all speculation. In short, his whole history was like a dream to the world, and no man can tell how or why he was awakened from the reverie.

Such is a faint and feeble picture of Napoleon Bonaparte, the first (and it is to be hoped the last) emperor of the French.

That he has done much evil there is little doubt; that he has been the origin of much good, there is just as little. Through his means, intentional or not, Spain, Portugal, and France have arisen to the blessings of a free constitution; superstition has found her grave in the ruins of the inquisition, and the feudal system, with its whole train of tyrannic satellites, has fled for ever. Kings may learn from him that their safest study, as well as their noblest, is the interest of the people; the people are taught by him that there is no despotism so stupendous against which they have not a resource; and to those who would rise upon the ruins of both, he is a living lesson, that if ambition can raise them from the lowest station, it can also prostrate them from the highest.

VI—1

LORD PLUNKET

ON CATHOLIC RELIEF [1]

(1821)

Born in 1765, died in 1854; entered the Irish Parliament in 1798;
opposed the " Union"; one of Emmet's prosecutors in 1803; Solicitor-
General for Ireland in Pitt's Cabinet in 1804; elected to Parliament
in 1812; raised to the Peerage in 1827; Lord Chancellor of Ireland,
1830–34 and 1835–41.

SIR, I hold in my hand a petition, signed by a
very considerable number of his majesty's Roman Catholic subjects of Ireland. A similar petition was presented, from the same body, the
year before last. It is unnecessary for me to remind the House that, on that occasion, it was presented by the late Mr. Grattan. It was sanctioned by the authority of his name, and en-
forced by all the resistless powers which waited
on the majesty of his genius. I have no design
to give vent to the feelings with which my heart
is filled, or to mingle with the public mourning
the mere peculiar and selfish regrets, which have
followed to the grave the friend by whose confidence I was honored, by whose wisdom I was

---

[1] From a speech in the House of Commons, February 28, 1821,
Plunket having succeeded after Grattan's death to leadership in the
Catholic cause. Peel said of this speech that "it stands nearly the
highest in point of ability of any ever heard in this House." Printed
here by kind permission of Messrs. James Duffy & Co., of Dublin.

instructed, by whose example I was guided. His eulogium has been heard from the lips of kindred eloquence and genius. The last duties have been rendered to his tomb by the gratitude and justice of the British people. In his death, as in his life, he has been a bond of connection between the countries.

I will not weaken the force of that eulogium, or disturb the solemnity of those obsequies, by my feeble praise, or unavailing sorrow; but with respect to the sentiments of that great and good man on this particular question, I wish to say a word. Sir, he had meditated upon it deeply and earnestly—it had taken early and entire possession of his mind, and held it to the last. He would willingly have closed his career of glory in the act of asserting within these walls the liberties of his countrymen; but still, regarding them as connected with the strength, the concord, and the security of the empire. Sir, he was alive to fame—to the fame that follows virtue. The love of it clung to him to the last moments of his life; but tho he felt that "last infirmity of noble minds," never did there breathe a human being who had a more lofty disdain for the shallow and treacherous popularity which is to be courted by subserviency, and purchased at the expense of principle and duty. He felt that this question was not to be carried as the triumph of a party or of a sect, but to be pursued as a great measure of public good, in which all were bound to forego their prejudices, and to humble their passions for the attainment of justice and of peace.

Our duty is to inquire whether injustice is offered to our fellow subjects, and if so, to atone for it; whether grievances press on them at which they have reason to be dissatisfied, and if so, to remove them; whether injurious distinctions exist, and if so, to obliterate them. If these things excite discontent, the more our shame to suffer injustice, and grievances, and injurious distinctions to remain, and the more imperious the call on every honorable mind to do them away.

Whatever difference of opinion exists on this subject, there is little of hostility, nothing of rancor. Prejudices, I must say, I believe there are; but when I call them so, I acknowledge them to be derived from an origin so noble, and to be associated with feelings so connected with the times when our civil and religious liberties were established, that they are entitled to a better name; and I am confident that they are accessible to reason and open to conviction, if met by the fair force of argument without rudeness and violence. Sir, it is impossible to mistake the feeling of the House and of the enlightened part of the country on this subject, or to doubt that it is a growing one.

And now, sir, I shall proceed, without further preface, to the main argument. The question presents itself in three distinct points of view: as a question of religion, as a question of constitutional principle, and as a question of policy and expediency, in reference to the stability of our existing establishments.

In the first place, it appears obvious that the requiring a religious pledge to the State, as a qualification for civil rights, makes religion an affair of state; because you can not lay it down as a rule to be applied only in a case of true religion, for every religion is the true one in the opinion of its own professors; and therefore, if the position is true in our instance, it must be equally true that, in every State, Protestant or Catholic, Christian or Pagan, the interests of true religion require a pledge to the State that the person admitted to its privileges is of the religion of that State. All this leads to the unavoidable inference that, in the opinion of those who so argue, there is no truth in any religion, and no criterion other than its adoption by the State. I do not say that such a principle may not be taken on trust by an honest man, and hotly insisted on by him, if he happens to be a zealous man, but I say it can not be deliberately and rationally maintained by any person who believes that there is any absolute truth in any religion.

Again, if religion is to be an affair of state, why not require some positive profession of faith as a qualification? Such as that he is a Christian, or that he believes in God, or in a future state, or that he has an immortal soul? Why does the declaration sound only in horror, and antipathy, and denunciation of another religion?

If the law is to be put into a state of electricity by the Church, why not of positive electricity?

Again; if we are to denounce, why denounce only one particular sect of Christians? Why not Socinians? Why not those who deny the divine nature of our Lord? Why select those who believe all that we do, merely because they believe something more? Why not Jews, Mohammedans, Pagans? Any one of these may safely make the declaration, provided he is willing to commit the breach of good manners which it requires. He may not only deny our God and our Redeemer, but he may worship Jupiter or Osiris, an ape or a crocodile, the host of heaven or the creeping things of the earth; let him only have a statutable horror of the religion of others, and agree to brand with the name of idolatry the religion of the greater part of the Christian world. But further, if the Roman Catholic religion is to be singled out as that, by the common bond of hatred to which we are all to be united in the ties of brotherly love and Christian charity, why select only one particular article of their faith, and say that the sacrifice of the Mass is impious and idolatrous? Why leave them their seven sacraments, their auricular confession, their purgatory; all equally badges of superstition, evidences of contumacy and causes of schism? Why make war exclusively upon this one article? We all declare solemnly that we consider the sacrifice of the Mass as superstitious and idolatrous. Now I entreat each member of this House to suppose that I am asking him individually, and as a private gentleman, does he know what is said, or meant, or done in the sacrifice of the Mass; or how it differs from our own mode of celebrating the Communion, so as to render it superstitious and idolatrous? If I could count upon the vote of every member, who must answer me that upon his honor he does not know, I should be sure of carrying, by an overwhelming majority, this or any other question I might think it proper to propose. Were I now to enter on a discussion of the nature of these doctrines, every member would complain that I was occupying the time of statesmen with subjects utterly unconnected with the business of the House or the policy of the country. Can there be a more decisive proof of its unsuitableness as a test?

By the Constitution of England, every liege subject is entitled, not merely to the protection of the laws, but is admissable to all the franchises and all the privileges of the State. For the argument I have now to deal with is this: "That by some principle of the Constitution, independent of the positive law, the Roman Catholic is necessarily excluded." What, then, is this principle of exclusion? Merely this, "that the Roman Catholics acknowledge the spiritual supremacy of the pope." Why then if, independently of the positive law, this acknowledgment deprives them of the privileges which belong to the liege subjects of the realm, the exclusive principle must have been in force before the law. If so,

167

there did not exist in England a liege man entitled to the privileges of the Constitution before the time of Henry the Eighth; for till then all acknowledged the spiritual supremacy of the pope. Magna Charta was established by outlaws from the State. Those gallant barons, whose descendants have been so feelingly alluded to by my noble friend, tho they were indeed permitted to achieve, yet were not entitled to share the liberties of their country. They might not dare to open the great charter which had been won by their hardihood and patriotism. Nay, more; if this principle be true, there is not, at this moment, a liege subject in any Catholic country in Europe. Sir, such trash as this shocks our common sense, and sets all argument at defiance.

I speak in the presence of enlightened constitutional lawyers and statesmen, and I do not fear a contradiction when I assert that the doctrine of exclusion is not to be found in the principles, or in the analogies of our Constitution, or in the history of our country, or in the opinion of any statesman whose name or memory has reached us. It is at once inconsistent with the subject's rights and with the king's prerogatives. Ours is a free monarchy, and it is of the essence of such a government that the king should be entitled to call for the services of all his liege subjects, otherwise it is not a monarchy; and that no class of his subjects should be excluded from franchise, otherwise it is not a free monarchy. I use the word franchise, not in the lawyers' tech-

nical sense of it, as a right supposed to be derived
by prescription or grant from the Crown, but in
the sense of Mr. Burke, when he applied it to
the right of voting for members to sit, and to the
right of sitting in Parliament. Sir, these are
privileges not derived from the grace of the
Crown or the permission of the Legislature, or
from the positive declaration of any written law,
but drawn from the great original sources from
which crown and law and legislature have been
derived; from the sacred fountains of British
Constitution and freedom; the denial of which,
as justified by any supposed principles of our
Constitution, I take on me to denounce as
founded on a radical ignorance of the essence
and stamina of our civil polity.

This principle of exclusion is equally at war
with the prerogative of the Crown and the title
of the subject. It wrests the scepter from the
king that it may strike at the liberties of the
people, and obtrudes an unconstitutional monopoly on the just rights of both. It is an insolent republican principle, which has more than
once been publicly and universally reprobated in
this House; the principle of lawless association,
for the purpose of lawless exclusion, and which
promises a conditional allegiance to the monarch,
so long only as he shall uphold the arrogant and
exclusive claims of one class of his subjects
against the inherent rights and privileges of the
other.

In all continued struggles between a lawful

government and a free people there can be but one issue. That party must prevail which has truth and justice on its side; otherwise there is an end of freedom or of government—it must end in despotism or anarchy. While you resist the claim of civil right, the Roman Catholic is armed with truth and justice. Grant him what he ought to have, and if he refuses the reasonable conditions or aspires to more, you transfer to yourselves these invincible standards, and you may look with confidence to the result.

Sir, to enumerate all the inconsistencies of this supposed measure of final adjustment would be endless; but there is one so glaring that I must beg leave particularly to allude to. You admit the Roman Catholic, both here and in Ireland, to the bar; you invite him to study the laws of his country, to display his knowledge on a public theater, where his talents and his acquirements are tried and known; you engage him in a career of honorable competition; you see him distinguished by the approbation of his countrymen; you see every relative connected with him gladdened and gratified by his successful progress; and when his heart is beating high with the consciousness of desert, and the hope of fame and honor, you stop him in his course, you dash his hopes, you extinguish his ambition, you leave him disgraced and mortified, sitting on the outer benches of your courts of justice, and imparting the gloom of his own hopeless exclusion to every one connected with him by consanguinity, friendship, or religion. Sir, in the name of the Protestant bar of both countries, I call on Parliament to rescue us from this disgrace, to relieve us from the odium and shame of this degrading monopoly, and to restore us to the privilege of equal and generous and honorable emulation.

One word more and I have done. It has been asked, where is concession to stop? I say, precisely where necessity, arising from public good, requires the continuance of the restriction. Exclusion is like war: *justum quibus necessarium.* Beyond this it would be folly to proceed. Short of this it is folly and injustice to stop. By this test let the claim be tried. If there is any office the possession of which by a Roman Catholic would be dangerous or injurious to our establishments, let him be excluded from it. If there is any franchise, whose exercise can be attended with real danger, let it be withheld. Such exclusion, or withholding, is not an anomaly, or inconsistency, in our system of conciliation, because, when the exclusion is not arbitrary and gratuitous, there is no insult. Such an exclusion forms no link of the chain, and the Roman Catholic will submit to it cheerfully; just as it would be the duty of the Protestant if, for similar reasons, a similar sacrifice were required from him. Let him know, in intelligible terms, the reason and the necessity, and he is satisfied. But do not, in so momentous a concern, give him words, and think to reconcile him. Talk to him of the Protestant establishment, and he understands you; he bows to it; he sees it engraved in capitals on the front of the political fabric. But if you tell him of Protestant ascendency, or Protestant exclusion, he asks in vain where its title is to be found; he looks in vain for it in the elements of our law or its traditions, in the commentaries of its sage expositors, in the Reformation, the Revolution, or the Union—he sees in it nothing but insult and contumacy; and he demands, in the name of the laws, and in the spirit of the Constitution, that he may be no longer its victim.

SHEIL

I

ON THE IRISH AS "ALIENS"[1]
(1837)

Born in 1791, died in 1851; admitted to Irish Bar, 1814; one of the founders of the Catholic Association, 1823, supporting O'Connell's movement for emancipation; elected to Parliament, 1829, and again 1831; Vice-President Board of Trade, 1839; Master of the Mint, 1846; British Minister in Florence, 1850.

I SHOULD be surprised, indeed, if, while you are doing us wrong, you did not profess your solicitude to do us justice. From the day on which Strongbow set his foot upon the shore of Ireland, Englishmen were never wanting in protestations of their deep anxiety to do us justice. Even Strafford, the deserter of the people's cause—the renegade Wentworth, who gave evidence in Ireland of the spirit of instinctive tyranny which predominated in his character—even Strafford, while he trampled upon our rights, and trod

---

[1] Delivered in the House of Commons February 23, 1837, the occasion being a debate on the Irish Municipal Bill. The passage here given was prompted by a remark made a few days before in the House of Lords, by Lord Lyndhurst, who referred to the Irish as "aliens in blood and religion." Lord Lyndhurst happened to be present in the House when Sheil rose to speak. Sheil pointed indignantly at him, which caused every member to turn his eyes on Lyndhurst, while shouts arose from the two sides and continued for some minutes.

upon the heart of the country, protested his solicitude to do justice to Ireland! What marvel
is it, then, that gentlemen opposite should deal in
such vehement protestations?

There is, however, one man of great abilities—
not a member of this House, but whose talents and
whose boldness have placed him in the topmost
place in his party—who, disdaining all imposture, and thinking it the best course to appeal
directly to the religious and national antipathies
of the people of this country,—abandoning all
reserve, and flinging off the slender veil by which
his political associates affect to cover, altho
they can not hide, their motives,—distinctly and
audaciously tells the Irish people that they are
not entitled to the same privileges as Englishmen; and pronounces them, in any particular
which could enter his minute enumeration of the
circumstances by which fellow citizenship is created, in race, identity and religion, to be aliens;
—to be aliens in race, to be aliens in country, to
be aliens in religion! Aliens! good God! was
Arthur, Duke of Wellington, in the House of
Lords,—and did he not start up and exclaim,
"HOLD, I HAVE SEEN THE ALIENS DO THEIR DUTY!"

The Duke of Wellington is not a man of an ex-
citable temperament. His mind is of a cast too
martial to be easily moved; but, notwithstanding
his habitual inflexibility, I can not help thinking
that, when he heard his Roman Catholic countrymen (for we are his countrymen) designated
by a phrase as offensive as the abundant vocabu-

lary of his eloquent confederate could supply,—
I can not help thinking that he ought to have
recollected the many fields of fight in which we
have been contributors to his renown. "The
battles, sieges, fortunes that he has passed,"
ought to have come back upon him. He ought to
have remembered that, from the earliest achievement in which he displayed that military genius
which has placed him foremost in the annals of
modern warfare, down to that last and surpassing combat which has made his name imperish-
able—from Assaye to Waterloo—the Irish soldiers, with whom your armies are filled, were the
inseparable auxiliaries to the glory with which
his unparalleled successes have been crowned.

Whose were the arms that drove your bayonets
at Vimiéra through the phalanxes that never
reeled in the shock of war before? What desperate valor climbed the steeps and filled the
moats at Badajos? All his victories should have
rushed and crowded back upon his memory—
Vimiéra, Badajos, Salamanca, Albuéra, Toulouse,
and, last of all, the greatest ——. Tell me—for
you were there—I appeal to the gallant soldier
before me [Sir Henry Harding], from whose
opinions I differ, but who bears, I know, a generous heart in an intrepid breast;—tell me—for
you must needs remember—on that day when
the destinies of mankind were trembling in the
balance, while death fell in showers, when the
artillery of France was leveled with a precision
of the most deadly science, when her legions, in-

cited by the voice and inspired by the example of their mighty leader, rushed again and again to the onset;—tell me if, for an instant, when to hesitate for an instant was to be lost, the "aliens" blenched?

And when, at length, the moment for the last and decided movement had arrived, and the valor which had so long been wisely checked was, at last, let loose,—when, with words familiar, but immortal, the great captain commanded the great assault,—tell me if Catholic Ireland with less heroic valor than the natives of this your own glorious country precipitated herself upon the foe? The blood of England, Scotland, and of Ireland, flowed in the same stream, and drenched the same field. When the chill morning dawned, their dead lay cold and stark together;—in the same deep pit their bodies were deposited; the green corn of spring is now breaking from their commingled dust; the dew falls from Heaven upon their union in the grave. Partakers in every peril, in the glory shall we not be permitted to participate; and shall we be told, as a requital, that we are estranged from the noble country for whose salvation our life-blood was poured out?

II

ON THE DISABILITIES OF THE JEWS [1]
(1848)

THAT men subject to all the duties should be deemed unworthy of the rights of Englishmen appears to me to be a remarkable anomaly. The enjoyment of rights ought not to be dissociated from the liabilities to duties. A British subject ought in every regard to be considered a British citizen; and inasmuch as the professors of the most ancient religion in the world, which, as far as it goes, we not only admit to be true, but hold to be the foundation of our own, are bound to the performance of every duty which attaches to a British subject, to a full fruition of every right which belongs to a British citizen, they have, I think, an irrefragable title. A Jew born in England can not transfer his allegiance from his sovereign and his country; if he were to enter the service of a foreign power engaged in hostilities with England and were taken in arms he would be accounted a traitor. Is a Jew an Englishman for no other purposes than those of condemnation? I am not aware of a single obligation to which other Englishmen are liable from

[1] Delivered in the House of Commons on February 7, 1848, when the election of Baron Rothschild to Parliament had revived the hopes of Jewish emancipation. It was not until 1858 that the Jewish disabilities were entirely removed. Abridged.

which a Jew is exempt; and if his religion confers on him no sort of immunity it ought not to affect him with any kind of disqualification.

It has been said in the course of these discussions that a Jew is not subject to penalties, but to privations. But what is privation but a synonym for penalty? Privation of life, privation of liberty, privation of property, privation of country, privation of right, privation of privilege—these are degrees widely distant indeed, but still degrees in the graduated scale of persecution. The parliamentary disability that affects the Jew has been designated in the course of these debates by the mollified expressions to which men who impart euphemism to severity are in the habit of resorting; but most assuredly an exclusion from the House of Commons ought in the House of Commons itself to be regarded as a most grievous detriment. With the dignity and the greatness and the power of this, the first assembly in the world, the hardship of exclusion is commensurate.

Some of the most prominent opponents of this measure are among the last by whom a seat in Parliament ought to be held in little account. On this branch of the case—the hardship of an exclusion from this House—I can speak as a witness as well as an advocate. I belong to that great and powerful community which was a few years ago subject to the same disqualification that affects the Jew, and I felt that disqualification to be most degrading. Of myself I will not speak, because I can speak of the most illustrious person by whom that community was adorned. I have sat under the gallery of the House of Commons by the side of Mr. O'Connell during a great discussion on which the destiny of Ireland was dependent. I was with him when Plunket convinced, and Brougham surprised, and Canning charmed, and Peel instructed, and Russell exalted and improved. How have I seen him repine at his exclusion from the field of high intellectual encounter in those lists in which so many competitors for glory were engaged, and into which, with an injurious tardiness, he was afterward admitted! How have I seen him chafe the chain which bound him down, but which, with an effort of gigantic prowess, he burst at last to pieces! He was at the head of millions of an organized and indissoluble people. The Jew comes here with no other arguments than those which reason and truth supply; but reason and truth are of counsel with him; and in this assembly, which I believe to represent not only the high intelligence but the high-mindedness of England, reason will not long be baffled, and truth, in fulfilment of its great aphorism, will at last prevail.

I will assume that the exclusion from this House is a great privation, and I proceed to consider whether it be not a great wrong. Nothing but necessity could afford its justification; and of this plea we should be taught, by a phrase which has almost grown proverbial, to beware.

Cardinal Caraffa relied upon necessity when he founded that celebrated tribunal whose practises are denounced by you, but upon whose maxims have a care lest you should unconsciously proceed. The sophistications of intolerance are refuted by their inconsistencies. If a Jew can choose, wherefore should he not be chosen? If a Jew can vote for a Christian, why should not a Christian vote for a Jew? Again, the Jew is admissable to the highest municipal employments; a Jew can be high sheriff—in other words, he can impanel the jury by which the first Christian commoner in England may be tried for his life.

But if necessity is to be pleaded as a justification for the exclusion of the Jew it must be founded on some great peril which would arise from his admission. What is it you fear? What is the origin of this Hebrewphobia? Do you tremble for the Church? The Church has something perhaps to fear from eight millions of Catholics and from three millions of Methodists and more than a million of Scotch seceders. The Church may have something to fear from the assault of sectaries from without, and still more to fear from a sort of spurious popery and the machinations of mitered mutiny from within; but from the synagog—the neutral, impartial, apathetic, and unproselytizing synagog—the Church has nothing to apprehend. But it is said that the House will become unchristianized. The Christianity of the Parliament depends on the Christianity of the country; and the Christianity

of the country is fixed in the faith and insepa-
rably intertwined with the affections of the people. It is as stable as England herself, and as long
as Parliament shall endure, while the Constitution shall stand, until the great mirror of the nation's mind shall have been shattered to pieces,
the religious feelings of the country will be faithfully reflected here. This is a security far better
than can be supplied by a test which presents a
barrier to an honest Jew, but which a scornful
skeptic can so readily and so disdainfully over-
leap.

Reference has been made in the course of these
discussions to the author of "The Decline and
Fall of the Roman Empire." A name still more
illustrious[1] might have been cited. Was not the
famous St. John—was not Bolingbroke, the fa-
tally accomplished, the admirable of the admirable, to whom genius paid an almost idolatrous
homage, and by whom a sort of fascination was
exercised over all those who had the misfortune
to approach him—was not the unhappy skeptic,
by whom far more mischief to religion and morality must have been done than could be effected
by half a hundred of the men by whom the Old
Testament is exclusively received, a member of
this House? Was he stopped by the test that
arrests the Jew; or did he not trample upon it
and ascend through this House to a sort of mas-

---

[1] This comparison, at the expense of Gibbon, is curious, as show-
ing how the reputation of Bolingbroke in 1848 still remained potent.

terdom in England and become the confidential and favorite adviser of his sovereign? He was not only an avowed and ostentatious infidel, but he was swayed by a distempered and almost insane solicitude for the dissemination of his disastrous disbelief.

Is it not then preposterous that a man by whom all revealed religion is repudiated, who doubts the immortality of the soul, doubts a future state of rewards and punishments, doubts in a superintending Providence, believes in nothing, fears nothing, and hopes for nothing, without any incentive to virtue, and without any restraint upon depravity excepting such as a sense of conventional honor or the promptings of a natural goodness may have given him—is it not, I say, preposterous, and almost monstrous, that such a man, for whom a crown of deadly nightshade should be woven, should be enabled, by playing the imposture of a moment and uttering a valueless formula at the table of the House, to climb to the pinnacle of power; and that you should slap the doors of this House with indignity upon a conscientious man who adheres to the faith in which he was born and bred; who believes in the great facts that constitute the foundation of Christianity; who believes in the perpetual existence of the nobler portion of our being; who believes in future retribution and in recompense to come; who believes that the world is taken care of by its almighty and everlasting Author; who believes in the mercy of God and practises humanity to man; who fulfils the ten great injunctions in which all morality is comprised; whose ear was never deaf to the supplications of the suffering; whose hand is as open as day to charity; and whose life presents an exemplification of the precepts of the Gospel far more faithful than that of many a man by whom, in the name of the Gospel, his dishonoring and unchristian disabilities are most wantonly, most injuriously, and most opprobriously maintained?

But where in the Scripture—in what chapter, in what text, in what single phrase—will you find an authority for resorting to the infliction of temporal penalty, or of temporal privation of any kind, as a means of propagating heavenly truth? You may find an authority, indeed, in the writings of jurists and of divines, and in the stern theology of those austere and haughty churchmen by whom the Pharisaical succession, far better than the Apostolical, is personally and demonstratively proved. But you will not find it in the New Testament; you will not find it in Matthew, nor in Mark, nor in Luke, nor in John, nor in the epistles of the meek and humble men to whom the teaching of all nations was given in charge; above all, you will not find in it anything that was ever said, or anything that was ever done, or anything that was ever suffered, by the Divine Author of the Christian religion, who spoke the Sermon on the Mountain, who said that the merciful should be blessed, and who, instead of ratifying the anathema which the people of

Jerusalem had invoked upon themselves, prayed
for forgiveness for those who knew not what they
did in consummating the sacrifice that was offered up for the transgressions of the world.

It was not by persecution, but despite of it—
despite of imprisonment, and exile, and spoliation, and shame, and death, despite the dungeon,
the wheel, the bed of steel, and the couch of fire—
that the Christian religion made its irresistible
and superhuman way. And is it not repugnant
to common reason, as well as to the elementary
principles of Christianity itself, to hold that it is
to be maintained by means diametrically the reverse of those by which it was propagated and
diffused? But, alas! for our frail and fragile nature, no sooner had the professors of Christianity
become the copartners of secular authority than
the severities were resorted to which their persecuted predecessors had endured. The Jew was
selected as an object of special and peculiar infliction.

The history of that most unhappy people is,
for century after century, a trail of chains and a
track of blood. Men of mercy occasionally arose
to interpose in their behalf. St. Bernard—the
great St. Bernard, the last of the Latin Fathers
—with a most pathetic eloquence took their part.
But the light that gleamed from the ancient turrets of the Abbey of Clairvaux was transitory
and evanescent. New centuries of persecution
followed; the Reformation did nothing for the
Jew. The infallibility of Geneva was sterner

than the infallibility of Rome. But all of us—Calvinists, Protestants, Catholics—all of us who have torn the seamless garment into pieces have sinned most fearfully in this terrible regard.

It is, however, some consolation to know that in Roman Catholic countries expiation of this guilt has commenced. In France and in Belgium all civil distinction between the Protestant and the Jew is at an end. To this Protestant country a great example will not have been vainly given. There did exist in England a vast mass of prejudice upon this question, which is, however, rapidly giving way. London, the point of imperial centralization, has made a noble manifestation of its will. London has advisedly, deliberately, and with benevolence aforethought selected the most prominent member of the Jewish community as its representative and united him with the first minister of the Crown. Is the Parliament prepared to fling back the Jew upon the people in order that the people should fling back the Jew upon the Parliament? That will be a dismal game, in the deprecation of whose folly and whose evils the Christian and the statesman should concur.

There exists in this country a most laudable anxiety for the conversion of the Jews. Meetings are held and money is largely subscribed for the purpose; but all these creditable endeavors will be ineffectual unless we make a restitution of his birthright to every Englishman who professes the Jewish religion. I know that

there are those who think that there is no such
thing as an English, or a French, or a Spanish
Jew. A Jew is but a Jew; his nationality, it is
said, is engrossed by the hand of recollection and
of hope, and the house of Jacob must remain
for ever in a state of isolation among the strange
people by whom it is encompassed. In answer
to these sophistries I appeal to human nature. It
is not wonderful that when the Jew was oppressed and pillaged and branded in a captivity
worse than Babylonian, he should have felt upon
the banks of the Thames, or of the Seine, or the
Danube, as his forefathers felt by the waters of
the Euphrates, and that the psalm of exile should
have found an echo in his heart. This is not
strange; it would have been strange if it had
been otherwise; but justice—even partial justice—has already operated a salutary change.

In the same manner in which we have relaxed
the laws against the Jews, that patriot instinct by
which we are taught to love the land of our birth
has been revived. British feeling has already
taken root in the heart of the Jew, and for its
perfect development nothing but perfect justice
is required. To the fallacies of fanaticism give
no heed. Emancipate the Jew—from the statute-
book of England be the last remnant of intolerance erased for ever; abolish all civil discrimina-
tions between the Christian and the Jews; fill his
whole heart with the consciousness of country.
Do this, and we dare be sworn that he will think
and feel and fear and hope as you do; his sorrow

and his exultation will be the same; at the tidings of English glory his heart will beat with a kindred palpitation; and whenever there shall be need, in the defense of his sovereign and of his country, his best blood, at your bidding, will be poured out with the same heroic prodigality as your own.

ISAAC BUTT

AT THE BAR OF THE HOUSE OF LORDS[1]
(1840)

Born in 1813, died in 1879; Editor of the *Dublin University Magazine* 1836-1838; noted as a lawyer; elected to Parliament in 1852; defended the Fenians 1865-69; elected to Parliament 1871, where he remained leader of the Home Rule party until 1877.

My duty is to endeavor to show to your lordships reasons why you ought not to adopt the provisions of the Bill now before your lordships for regulating the municipalities of Ireland, so far as they destroy the rights, confiscate the property, and abrogate the charters of the City of Dublin.

The petitions which have been presented, my lords, briefly state the case. Your lordships will perceive that it is a case involving both private rights and public interests; and I do confess that this very circumstance makes me feel no little embarrassment in addressing you. My lords, I will first call your attention to this Bill as divided into two parts: it is a Bill of disfranchisement, and a Bill of enfranchisement. It begins by sweeping away every existing right

[1] From his speech at the Bar of the House of Lords May 15, 1840. Mr. Butt, who was then a noted leader at the Irish Bar, had been selected by the Corporation of Dublin as the junior barrister to make this plea.

in the City of Dublin. Not the right of a single
freeman to vote for municipal offices is retained.
No privilege is spared—no franchise respected.
However your lordships may decide as to the admission to new rights and new franchises, we
fearlessly assert that no reason has yet been
supplied which can justify you as the highest
court of judicature in the land in forfeiting the
existing right of freemen. Thus, my lords, our
first ground of protesting against this Bill is
that of individual injustice. You punish a number of individuals who have been advanced under
the existing order of things to the highest offices
in the magistracy of the city; I say you punish,
because to degrade is to punish. You degrade, in
the evening of their days, the aldermen—men
who have borne an unblemished character, who,
as magistrates, have never yet been charged with
partiality in the execution of their magisterial
duties; you degrade the sheriff's peers, who have
acquired their right by long and onerous attention to several duties; and you degrade the freemen of the City of Dublin, because you take from
them their rights—rights which have hitherto
been supposed to rest upon the same foundation
as the privileges of your lordships' illustrious
House—upon hereditary succession, the transmission from father to son, upon the charters of
monarchs, and upon repeated acts of Parliament
recognizing their privileges. I do again and
again urge upon your lordships' justice this one
broad principle of the Constitution, that by the

law of England no man can be punished unless he
is convicted of a crime; that when you degrade,
you punish; that when you take away franchise,
you punish; and that, therefore, this is a bill
inflicting punishment upon parties against whom
not merely no crime has been proved, but against
whom no charge even has been made.

The only proper municipal function which this
Dublin Corporation will have to discharge, with
its enormous revenue and power of taxation, is to
supply us with cold water; and perhaps, my
learned friend would say, by agitation keep us in
hot water, too. For this large amount of taxation
we are to get nothing in return. It is to be
solely applied to the payment of officers; to keep
up an expensive staff for a body whose only
business will be political agitation. The very
absence of all useful occupation compels them to
seek employment the reverse of useful. You
create a corporation which you call municipal,
and then studiously shut it out from every
municipal function; you will not let them light a
lamp; you will not permit them to pave a street;
you have provided us a separate police, one man
of which they can not control. You have given
them great pomp—"The Right Honorable, the
Lord Mayor and the Aldermen," with their
chains, their collars and their gowns. I do not
speak lightly of these emblems of civic authority.
You invest this new body with all the prestige
of ancient authority. Is it to be expected that
a corporation you have enthroned in dignity will

sink down into insignificance and do nothing? But their choice is between insignificance and mischief. If they do not become political agitators, they have nothing to do. In the name of the great mass of the professional inhabitants of Dublin, I ask for what you will impose on us the tyranny of this body? We have no objection to the present corporation: it does not tax us; it does not interfere with us; it does not agitate against our religion—against the Church we love—the laws we revere—and the Constitution we are determined to uphold; we are content to pursue our vocations at our profession and have nothing to do with it. But this new corporation will do all these things, while it has no one useful function to discharge. You are incorporating some one of those seditious societies in Dublin which for years have convulsed the peace of the country, and made it difficult for any good government to be established. This Act is utterly useless for municipal purposes; it is an Act to incorporate the Trades Union, give them the power to legislate and to tax with perpetual succession, by the name of lord mayor, aldermen, and burgesses.

Now, my lords, the point we have urged in our petition is, that Dublin ought to be exempt, as you have exempted London; that, whatever regulations you may hereafter apply to us, you can not deal with Dublin upon the principle of establishing a purely democratic corporation. In our petition we state our willingness to acquiesce in any measure of reform that your lordships can adopt that will not compromise the safety of the Protestant religion or violate our charters; but, my lords, by adopting this measure you will do grievous injustice to the population of a metropolitan city. Why subject us to the control of a democratic corporation, with which we have no sympathy, no unity of sentiment, no connection, no influence? Why place the bar, the professional classes, the gentry of Ireland, under the control of the populace of its chief city? The principle has never been carried into effect in England. I do not merely urge that London has been exempted; but what would your lordships say if it was proposed to incorporate into one vast corporation the whole of this immense metropolis, so that Finsbury Square should give law to St. James's? Is it because the professional classes and gentry of Dublin are distant, because they are unprotected, that you will inflict upon them a grievance and tyranny which you would not endure in London? I may be told that you must give the same Bill to Ireland that you have given to England, no matter how differently circumstanced the two countries. I take the argument. I say, if you give us all the evil, give us the one solitary good. London has been exempted— exempt Dublin. You have respected the Magna Charta of John in London; why not respect the Magna Charta of Henry in Dublin? Am I to be told that, because on the faith of England we gave up our independent Parliament, that you are to disregard us? On the faith of the legislative union, my lords, we demand that our rights should be held in the same respect as those of London. In our own Parliament they were so. Once, indeed, in that Parliament, in a debate upon the privileges of the City of Dublin, it was pleaded that some similar rights of the City of London had been respected by the English legislature. Some one dared to hint that the privileges of Dublin stood on lower and less sacred grounds. Who was the man who rose with prompt indignation to resent this insult to the Constitution of Ireland?—a man, my lords, whose memory is still held in honor in our country—the illustrious Henry Grattan! He it was who, in the spirit of a true Irishman, indignantly denounced the attempt to place the privileges of Dublin below those of London. It was no part of that great man's patriotism to vilify and bring into contempt the institutions of his country.

There is, indeed, my lords, a people who look with intense anxiety to your decision on this question—the people to whom these charters were granted, the Protestant people of Ireland. They contemplate this Bill with alarm and dismay; they believe that it will place them under a tyranny intolerant and intolerable—that it will hand over their country to the control of Jacobin clubs, but Jacobinism on which will be engrafted the worst elements of national antipathy and

religious hate; which will present to the world
the spectacle of the extraordinary influence of
civil anarchy and religious despotism, uniting
in an anomalous combination all the evils of
democracy and of superstition. They implore
of your lordships to protect them from this
tyranny. One argument they have against this
measure which your lordships will not disregard.
In this the highest court of judicature in the
realm, where the errors of every inferior tribunal
are corrected—in · this most solemn and most
honorable of all tribunals, they appeal with confidence to your lordships, and say that this
measure ought not to pass because it is unjust.

My lords, I have done. For myself I have no
words strong enough to express my gratitude
for the patience and indulgence with which you
have heard me. If in any thing I may have wan-
dered beyond the limits which my situation imposed, I implore of your lordships to attribute
it to the embarrassment and novelty of my position—my inexperience in the forms and usages
of your lordships' House.

O'CONNELL

IN FAVOR OF THE REPEAL OF
THE UNION [1]

(1843)

Born in 1775, died in 1847; founded the Catholic Association in 1823, and became a leader in the agitation for Catholic emancipation; elected to Parliament in 1828; a leader in the Repeal agitation in 1840; promoted the mass-meetings of 1842-43; arrested and convicted of conspiracy and sedition in 1843; his sentence reversed in 1844.

I ACCEPT with the greatest alacrity the high honor you have done me in calling me to the chair of this majestic meeting. I feel more honored than I ever did in my life, with one single exception, and that related to, if possible, an equally majestic meeting at Tara. But I must say that if a comparison were instituted between them, it would take a more discriminating eye than mine to discover any difference between them. There are the same incalculable numbers; there is the same firmness; there is the same

[1] Delivered at Mullaghmast, Ireland, in September, 1843. Since 1829 agitation in Ireland for repeal had been in progress, and since 1842 had been rapidly intensified, until in the spring of 1843 a series of monster meetings had been started at Trim. Estimates of the multitude assembled on the Hill of Tara in August vary from 150,000 to 1,000,000. In the speech here given, O'Connell says that the multitude at Mullaghmast rivaled the one at Tara.

determination; there is the same exhibition of love to old Ireland; there is the same resolution not to violate the peace; not to be guilty of the slightest outrage; not to give the enemy power by committing a crime, but peacefully and manfully to stand together in the open day, to protest before man and in the presence of God against the iniquity of continuing the Union.

At Tara I protested against the Union—I repeat the protest at Mullaghmast. I declare solemnly my thorough conviction as a constitutional lawyer, that the Union is totally void in point of principle and of constitutional force. I tell you that no portion of the empire had the power to traffic on the rights and liberties of the Irish people. The Irish people nominated them to make laws, and not legislatures. They were appointed to act under the Constitution, and not annihilate it. Their delegation from the people was confined within the limits of the Constitution, and the moment the Irish Parliament went beyond those limits and destroyed the Constitution, that moment it annihilated its own power, but could not annihilate the immortal spirit of liberty which belongs, as a rightful inheritance, to the people of Ireland. Take it, then, from me that the Union is void.

I admit there is the force of a law, because it has been supported by the policeman's truncheon, by the soldier's bayonet, and by the horseman's sword; because it is supported by the courts of law and those who have power to adjudicate in them; but I say solemnly, it is not supported by constitutional right. The Union, therefore, in my thorough conviction, is totally void, and I avail myself of this opportunity to announce to several hundreds of thousands of my fellow subjects that the Union is an unconstitutional law and that it is not fated to last long—its hour is approaching. America offered us her sympathy and support. We refused the support, but we accepted the sympathy; and while we accepted the sympathy of the Americans, we stood upon the firm ground of the right of every human being to liberty; and I, in the name of the Irish nation, declare that no support obtained from America should be purchased by the price of abandoning principle for one moment, and that principle is that every human being is entitled to freedom.

My friends, I want nothing for the Irish but their country, and I think the Irish are competent to obtain their own country for themselves. I like to have the sympathy of every good man everywhere, but I want not armed support or physical strength from any country. The Republican party in France offered me assistance. I thanked them for their sympathy, but I distinctly refused to accept any support from them. I want support from neither France nor America, and if that usurper, Louis Philippe, who trampled on the liberties of his own gallant nation, thought fit to assail me in his newspaper, I returned the taunt with double vigor, and I denounce him to Europe and the world as a treacherous tyrant, who has violated the compact with his own country, and therefore is not fit to assist the liberties of any other country.

I want not the support of France; I want not the support of America; I have physical support enough about me to achieve any change; but you know well that it is not my plan—I will not risk the safety of one of you. I could not afford the loss of one of you—I will protect you all, and it is better for you all to be merry and alive, to enjoy the repeal of the Union; but there is not a man of you there that would not, if we were attacked unjustly and illegally, be ready to stand in the open field by my side. Let every man that concurs in that sentiment lift up his hand.[1]

The assertion of that sentiment is our sure protection; for no person will attack us, and we will attack nobody. Indeed, it would be the height of absurdity for us to think of making any attack; for there is not one man in his senses, in Europe or America, that does not admit that the repeal of the Union is now inevitable. The English papers taunted us, and their writers laughed us to scorn; but now they admit that it is impossible to resist the application for repeal. More power to you. But that even shows we have power enough to know how to use it. Why, it is only this week that one of the leading London newspapers, called the *Morning Herald*,

[1] In reference to this appeal it is recorded that in that vast audience all hands were lifted up.

which had a reporter at the Lismore meeting, published an account of that great and mighty meeting, and in that account the writer expressly says that it will be impossible to refuse so peaceable, so determined, so unanimous a people as the people of Ireland the restoration of their domestic legislature.

For my own part, I would have thought it wholly unnecessary to call together so large a meeting as this, but for the trick played by Wellington, and Peel, and Graham, and Stanley, and the rest of the paltry administration, by whose government this country is disgraced. I do not suppose so worthless an administration ever before got together. Lord Stanley is a renegade from Whiggism, and Sir James Graham is worse. Sir Robert Peel has five hundred colors on his bad standard, and not one of them is permanent. To-day it is orange, to-morrow it will be green, the day after neither one nor the other, but we shall take care that it shall never be dyed in blood.

Then there is the poor old Duke of Wellington, and nothing was ever so absurd as their deification of him in England. The English historian —rather the Scotch one—Alison, an arrant Tory, admits that the Duke of Wellington was surprised at Waterloo, and if he got victoriously out of that battle, it was owing to the valor of the British troops and their unconquerable determination to die, but not to yield. No man is ever a good soldier but the man who goes into

the battle determined to conquer or not come
back from the battle-field. No other principle
makes a good soldier; conquer or die is the
battle-cry for the good soldier; conquer or die
is his only security. The Duke of Wellington
had troops at Waterloo that had learned that
word, and there were Irish troops among them.
You all remember the verses made by poor Shan
Van Vocht:

> "At famed Waterloo
> Duke Wellington would look blue
> If Paddy was not there too,
> Says the Shan Van Vocht."

Yes, the glory he got there was bought by the
blood of the English, Irish, and Scotch soldiers—
the glory was yours. He is nominally a member
of the administration, but yet they would not
intrust him with any kind of office. He has no
duty at all to perform, but a sort of Irish anti-
repeal warden. I thought I never would be
obliged to the ministry, but I am obliged to
them. They put a speech abusing the Irish into
the queen's mouth. They accused us of disaffection, but they lied; it is their speech; there is no
disaffection in Ireland. We were loyal to the
sovereigns of Great Britain, even when they
were our enemies; we were loyal to George III.,
even when he betrayed us; we were loyal to
George IV. when he blubbered and cried when
we forced him to emancipate us; we were loyal
to old Billy, tho his minister put into his

mouth a base, bloody, and intolerant speech against Ireland; and we are loyal to the queen, no matter what our enemies may say to the contrary. It is not the queen's speech, and I pronounce it to be a lie.

There is no dissatisfaction in Ireland, but there is this—a full determination to obtain justice and liberty. I am much obliged to the ministry for that speech, for it gives me, among other things, an opportunity of addressing such meetings as this. I had held the monster meetings. I had fully demonstrated the opinion of Ireland. I was convinced their unanimous determination to obtain liberty was sufficiently signified by the many meetings already held; but when the minister's speech came out, it was necessary to do something more. Accordingly, I called a monster meeting at Loughrea. I called another meeting in Cliffden. I had another monster meeting in Lismore, and here now we are assembled on the Rath of Mullaghmast.

O my friends, I will keep you clear of all treachery—there shall be no bargain, no compromise with England—we shall take nothing but repeal, and a Parliament in College Green. You will never, by my advice, confide in any false hopes they hold out to you; never confide in anything coming from them, or cease from your struggle, no matter what promise may be held to you, until you hear me say I am satisfied; and I will tell you where I will say that—near the statue of King William, in College Green. No;

we came here to express our determination to die to a man, if necessary, in the cause of old Ireland. We came to take advice of each other, and, above all, I believe you came here to take my advice. I can tell you, I have the game in my hand—I have the triumph secure—I have the repeal certain, if you but obey my advice.

I will go slow—you must allow me to do so—but you will go sure. No man shall find himself imprisoned or persecuted who follows my advice. I have led you thus far in safety; I have swelled the multitude of repealers until they are identified with the entire population, or nearly the entire population, of the land, for seven-eighths of the Irish people are now enrolling themselves repealers. I do not want more power; I have power enough; and all I ask of you is to allow me to use it. I will go on quietly and slowly, but I will go on firmly, and with a certainty of success. I am now arranging a plan for the formation of the Irish House of Commons.

It is a theory, but it is a theory that may be realized in three weeks. The repeal arbitrators are beginning to act; the people are submitting their differences to men chosen by themselves. You will see by the newspapers that Doctor Gray and my son, and other gentlemen, have already held a petty session of their own, where justice will be administered free of all expense to the people. The people shall have chosen magistrates of their own in the room of the magistrates who have been removed. The people shall submit their differences to them, and shall have strict justice administered to them that shall not cost them a single farthing. I shall go on with that plan until we have all the disputes settled and decided by justices appointed by the people themselves.

I wish to live long enough to have perfect justice administered to Ireland, and liberty proclaimed throughout the land. It will take me some time to prepare my plan for the formation of the new Irish House of Commons—that plan which we will yet submit to her majesty for her approval when she gets rid of her present paltry administration and has one that I can support. But I must finish that job before I go forth, and one of my reasons for calling you together is to state my intentions to you. Before I arrange my plan, the Conciliation Hall will be finished, and it will be worth any man's while to go from Mullaghmast to Dublin to see it.

When we have it arranged I will call together three hundred, as the *Times* called them, "bogtrotters," but better men never stepped on pavement. But I will have the three hundred, and no thanks to them. Wales is up at present, almost in a state of insurrection. The people there have found that the landlords' power is too great, and has been used tyrannically, and I believe you agree with them tolerably well in that. They insist on the sacredness of the right of the tenants to security of possession, and with the equity of tenure which I would establish we will do the landlords full justice, but we will do the people justice also. We will recollect that the land is the landlord's, and let him have the benefit of it, but we will also recollect that the labor belongs to the tenant, and the tenant must have the value of his labor, not transitory and by the day, but permanently and by the year.

Yes, my friends, for this purpose I must get some time. I worked the present repeal year tolerably well. I believe no one in January last would believe that we could have such a meeting within the year as the Tara demonstration. You may be sure of this—and I say it in the presence of Him who will judge me—that I never will wilfully deceive you. I have but one wish under heaven, and that is for the liberty and prosperity of Ireland. I am for leaving England to the English, Scotland to the Scotch; but we must have Ireland for the Irish. I will not be content until I see not a single man in any office, from the lowest constable to the lord chancellor, but Irishmen. This is our land, and we must have it. We will be obedient to the queen, joined to England by the golden link of the Crown, but we must have our own Parliament, our own bench, our own magistrates, and we will give some of the *shoneens* who now occupy the bench leave to retire, such as those lately appointed by Sugden. He is a pretty boy, sent here from England; but I ask: Did you ever hear such a name as he has got? I remember, in Wexford, a man told me he had a pig at home which he was

so fond of that he would call it Sugden. No; we
shall get judicial independence for Ireland. It
is for this purpose we are assembled here to-day,
as every countenance I see around me testifies.
If there is any one here who is for the Union, let
him say so. Is there anybody here for the repeal? [Cries of "All, all!"]

Yes, my friends, the Union was begot in iniquity—it was perpetuated in fraud and cruelty.
It was no compact, no bargain, but it was an act
of the most decided tyranny and corruption that
was ever yet perpetrated. Trial by jury was
suspended—the right of personal protection was
at an end—courts-martial sat throughout the
land—and the County of Kildare, among others,
flowed with blood. We shall stand peaceably
side by side in the face of every enemy. Oh,
how delighted was I in the scenes which I witnessed as I came along here to-day! How my
heart throbbed, how my spirit was elevated, how
my bosom swelled with delight at the multitude
which I beheld, and which I shall behold, of the
stalwart and strong men of Kildare! I was delighted at the activity and force that I saw
around me, and my old heart grew warm again
in admiring the beauty of the dark-eyed maids
and matrons of Kildare. Oh, there is a star-
light sparkling from the eye of a Kildare beauty
that is scarcely equaled, and could not be ex-
celled, all over the world. And remember that
you are the sons, the fathers, the brothers, and
the husbands of such women, and a traitor or a

coward could never be connected with any of them. Yes, I am in a county, remarkable in the history of Ireland for its bravery and its misfortune, for its credulity in the faith of others, for its people judged of the Saxon by the honesty and honor of their own natures. I am in a county celebrated for the sacredness of shrines and fanes. I am in a county where the lamp of Kildare's holy shrine burned with its sacred fire, through ages of darkness and storm—that fire which for six centuries burned before the high altar without being extinguished, being fed continuously, without the slightest interruption, and it seemed to me to have been not an inapt representation of the continuous fidelity and religious love of country of the men of Kildare.

Yes, you have those high qualities—religious fidelity, continuous love of country. Even your enemies admit that the world has never produced any people that exceeded the Irish in activity and strength. The Scottish philosopher has declared, and the French philosopher has confirmed it, that number one in the human race is, blessed be Heaven, the Irishman. In moral virtue, in religion, in perseverance, and in glorious temperance, you excel. Have I any teetotalers here? Yes, it is teetotalism that is repealing the Union. I could not afford to bring you together, I would not dare to bring you together, but that I had the teetotalers for my police.

Yes, among the nations of the earth, Ireland stands number one in the physical strength of her sons and in the beauty and purity of her daughters. Ireland, land of my forefathers, how my mind expands, and my spirit walks abroad in something of majesty, when I contemplate the high qualities, inestimable virtues, and true purity and piety and religious fidelity of the inhabitants of your green fields and productive mountains. Oh, what a scene surrounds us! It is not only the countless thousands of brave and active and peaceable and religious men that are here assembled, but Nature herself has written her character with the finest beauty in the verdant plains that surround us.

Let any man run around the horizon with his eye, and tell me if created nature ever produced anything so green and so lovely, so undulating, so teeming with production. The richest harvests that any land can produce are those reaped in Ireland; and then here are the sweetest meadows, the greenest fields, the loftiest mountains, the purest streams, the noblest rivers, the most capacious harbors—and her water power is equal to turn the machinery of the whole world. O my friends, it is a country worth fighting for—it is a country worth dying for; but, above all, it is a country worth being tranquil, determined, submissive, and docile for; disciplined as you are in obedience to those who are breaking the way, and trampling down the barriers between you and your constitutional liberty, I will see every man of you having a vote, and every man protected by the ballot from the agent or landlord.

I will see labor protected, and every title to possession recognized, when you are industrious and honest. I will see prosperity again throughout your land—the busy hum of the shuttle and the tinkling of the smithy shall be heard again. We shall see the nailer employed even until the middle of the night, and the carpenter covering himself with his chips. I will see prosperity in all its gradations spreading through a happy, contented, religious land. I will hear the hymn of a happy people go forth at sunrise to God in praise of His mercies—and I will see the evening sun set down among the uplifted hands of a religious and free population. Every blessing that man can bestow and religion can confer upon the faithful heart shall spread throughout the land. Stand by me—join with me—I will say be obedient to me, and Ireland shall be free.

MEAGHER

ON ABHORRING THE SWORD [1]
(1846)

Born in 1823, died in 1867; identified with the Irish Repeal Association in 1844; a member of the war directory of the Irish Confedera-
tion in 1848; transported to Van Diemen's Land in 1849; escaped to
New York in 1852; entered the Federal army in 1861; a Brigadier-
General in 1862; Governor of Montana in 1866.

A GOOD government may, indeed, redress the
grievances of an injured people; but a strong
people can alone build up a great nation. To be
strong, a people must be self-reliant, self-ruled,
self-sustained. The dependence of one people
upon another, even for the benefits of legislation,
is the deepest source of national weakness.

By an unnatural law it exempts a people from
their just duties,—their just responsibilities.
When you exempt a people from these duties,
from these responsibilities, you generate in them
a distrust in their own powers. Thus you ener-
vate, if you do not utterly destroy, that spirit
which a sense of these responsibilities is sure to
inspire, and which the fulfilment of these duties
never fails to invigorate. Where this spirit does

[1] The celebrated "Sword Speech," which was delivered in Constitution Hall, Dublin, July 20, 1846, when Meagher was not quite
twenty-three years of age. It was made as a protest against what
was then known as "trafficking with the Whigs." Abridged.

not actuate, the country may be tranquil—it will not be prosperous. It may exist—it will not thrive. It may hold together—it will not advance. Peace it may enjoy—for peace and serfdom are compatible. But, my lord, it will neither accumulate wealth, nor win a character. It will neither benefit mankind by the enterprise of its merchants, nor instruct mankind by the examples of its statesmen. I make these observations, for it is the custom of some moderate politicians to say, that when the Whigs have accomplished the "pacification" of the country, there will be little or no necessity for Repeal.

But the Whigs will enrich as well as pacify? Grant it, my lord. Then do I conceive that the necessity for Repeal will augment. Great interests demand great safeguards. The prosperity of a nation requires the protection of a senate. Hereafter a national senate may require the protection of a national army.

So much for the extraordinary affluence with which we are threatened; and which, it is said by gentlemen on the opposite shore of the Irish Sea, will crush this association and clamor for Irish nationality, in a sepulcher of gold. This prediction, however, is feebly sustained by the ministerial program that has lately appeared. After that most consolatory announcement, my lord, let those who have the patience of Job and the poverty of Lazarus, continue in good faith "to wait on Providence and the Whigs"—continue to entertain "some kind of hope" that if not "a complete and immediate remedy," at least "some remedy," "some improvement" will place this country in "a far better state" than it is at present, "some ten or twelve years hence." After that, let those who prefer the periodical boons of a Whig government to that which would be the abiding blessing of an Irish Parliament—let those who deny to Ireland what they assert for Poland—let those who would inflict, as Henry Grattan said, an eternal disability upon this country, to which Providence has assigned the largest facilities for power—let those who would ratify the "base swap," as Mr. Sheil once stigmatized the Act of Union, and would stamp perfection upon that deed of perfidy—let such men

> ——"Plod on in sluggish misery,
> Rotting from sire to sire, from age to age,
> Proud of their trampled nature."

But we, my lord, who are assembled in this hall, and in whose hearts the Union has not bred the slave's disease—we who have not been imperialized—we are here, with the hope to undo that work, which, forty-six years ago, dishonored the ancient peerage, and subjugated the people of our country.

My lord, to assist the people of Ireland to undo that work, I came to this hall. I came to repeal the Act of Union; I came here for nothing else. Upon every other question, I feel myself at perfect liberty to differ from each and every one of you. Upon questions of finance, questions of religious character, questions of an educational character, questions of municipal policy, questions that may arise from the proceedings of the legislature; upon all these questions, I feel myself at perfect liberty to differ from each and every one of you.

Yet more, my lord, I maintain that it is my right to express my opinion upon each of these questions, if necessary. The right of free discussion I have here upheld. In the exercise of that right I have differed, sometimes, from the leader of this association, and would do so again. That right I will not abandon—I shall maintain it to the last. In doing so, let me not be told that I seek to undermine the influence of the leader of this association and am insensible to his services. My lord, I am grateful for his services, and will uphold his just influence. This is the first time I have spoken in these terms of that illustrious man, in this hall. I did not do so before—I felt it was unnecessary. I hate unnecessary praise—I scorn to receive it, I scorn to bestow it.

No, my lord, I am not ungrateful to the man[1] who struck the fetters off my arms while I was yet a child, and by whose influence, my father—the first Catholic who did so for two hundred years—sat, for the last two years, in the civic chair of an ancient city. But, my lord, the same God who gave to that great man the power to strike down an odious ascendency in this coun-

[1] Daniel O'Connell.

try, and enable him to institute in this land the glorious law of religious equality; the same God gave to me a mind that is my own—a mind that has not been mortgaged to the opinions of any man or any set of men; a mind that I was to use, and not surrender. My lord, in the exercise of that right, which I have here endeavored to uphold—a right which this association should preserve inviolate, if it desires not to become a despotism—in the exercise of that right, I have differed from Mr. O'Connell on previous occasions, and differ from him now.

In the existing circumstances of the country an excitement to arms would be senseless and wicked because irrational. To talk nowadays of repealing the Act of Union by force of arms would be to rhapsodize. If the attempt were made it would be a decided failure. There might be a riot in the street—there would be no revolution in the country. The secretary, Mr. Crean, will far more effectually promote the cause of repeal, by registering votes in Green Street than registering firearms in the head police office. Conciliation Hall on Burg Quay is more impregnable than a rebel camp on Vinegar Hill. The hustings at Dundalk will be more successfully stormed than the magazine in the park. The registry club, the reading-room, the polling booths,—these are the only positions in the country we can occupy. Voters' certificates, books, pamphlets, newspapers,—these are the only weapons we can employ. Therefore, my lord, I cast my vote in favor of the peaceful policy of this association. It is the only policy we can adopt. If that policy be pursued with truth, with courage, with fixed determination of purpose, I firmly believe it will succeed.

But, my lord, I dissented from the resolutions before us for other reasons. I stated the first; I now come to the second. I dissented from them, for I felt that, by assenting to them, I should have pledged myself to the unqualified repudiation of physical force in all countries, at all times, and under every circumstance. This I could not do. For, my lord, I do not abhor the use of arms in the vindication of national rights. There are times when arms will alone suffice, and when political ameliorations call for a drop of blood, and many thousand drops of blood. Opinion, I admit, will operate against opinion. But, as the honorable member for Kilkenny has observed, force must be used against force. The soldier is proof against an argument, but he is not proof against a bullet. The man that will listen to reason, let him be reasoned with; but it is the weaponed arm of the patriot that can alone prevail against battalioned despotism.

Then, my lord, I do not condemn the use of arms as immoral, nor do I conceive it profane to say that the King of Heaven—the Lord of Hosts! the God of Battles! bestows His benediction upon those who unsheathe the sword in the hour of a nation's peril.

From that evening on which, in the valley of Bethulia, He nerved the arm of the Jewish girl to smite the drunken tyrant in his tent, down to this day, in which He has blessed the insurgent chivalry of the Belgian priest, His Almighty hand hath ever been stretched forth from His throne of light, to consecrate the flag of freedom, to bless the patriot's sword! Be it in the defense, or be it in the assertion of a people's liberty, I hail the sword as a sacred weapon; and if, my lord, it has sometimes taken the shape of the serpent and reddened the shroud of the oppressor with too deep a dye, like the anointed rod of the high priest, it has at other times, and as often, blossomed into celestial flowers to deck the freeman's brow.

Abhor the sword—stigmatize the sword? No, my lord, for, in the passes of the Tyrol, it cut to pieces the banner of the Bavarian, and, through those cragged passes, struck a path to fame for the peasant insurrectionist of Insprück! Abhor the sword—stigmatize the sword? No, my lord, for at its blow, a giant nation started from the waters of the Atlantic, and by its redeeming magic, and in the quivering of its crimson light, the crippled colony sprang into the attitude of a proud Republic—prosperous, limitless, and invincible! Abhor the sword—stigmatize the sword? No, my lord, for it swept the Dutch marauders out of the fine old towns of Belgium, scourged them back to their own phlegmatic swamps, and knocked their flag and scepter, their laws and bayonets, into the sluggish waters of the Scheldt.

My lord, I learned that it was the right of a nation to govern herself, not in this hall, but upon the ramparts of Antwerp. This, the first article of a nation's creed, I learned upon those ramparts, where freedom was justly estimated, and the possession of the precious gift was purchased by the effusion of generous blood. My lord, I honor the Belgians, I admire the Belgians, I love the Belgians, for their enthusiasm, their courage, their success, and I, for one, will not stigmatize, for I do not abhor, the means by which they obtained a citizen king, a chamber of deputies.[1]

[1] Here the speaker was interrupted and not being permitted to proceed, he and his friends left the hall and never entered it again.

A. M. SULLIVAN

ON THE ZULU WAR[1]

(1879)

Born in 1830, died in 1884; became Editor and Proprietor of the
Dublin Nation, 1846; opposed the Fenian Movement; ordered to
be assassinated, but the order never executed; imprisoned, 1868;
elected to Parliament as a Home Ruler, 1874; reelected, 1880, but
owing to ill health resigned, 1881; buried in the "O'Connell Circle"
in Glasnevin Cemetery.

WE find ourselves once again sitting in Committee of the Whole House to vote a war subsidy.
The present occupants of the Treasury Bench
are determined that so long as they retain their
places the Temple of Janus shall not be closed.
In the reading-room of this House, a couple of

---

[1] From a speech in the House of Commons, February 27, 1879. By
permission of Mr. T. D. Sullivan, brother of A. M. Sullivan. The circumstances in which this speech was delivered were described at
the time as follows, by the Parliamentary correspondent of the
Liverpool *Journal* : "But the debate was not to be wholly and un-
interruptedly dreary, for near the end of it there came a speech
from Mr. Sullivan, the member for Louth, which drove away all
dulness for the time, and lighted up the debate as a lightning flash
illuminates the sky on a murky night. The speech was short, but
the effect must have been startling. These people had been dro-
ning for several hours about mere money matters. Meanwhile Mr.
Sullivan sat in his place on the second bench from the floor below
the gangway. At last, when Sir Stafford had in his dryest style
delivered his winding-up speech, Sullivan's patience gave out, and
up he sprang, and, kicking all precedent aside, and knocking old
use and wont head over heels, he stormed into the debate like a
tornado."

years ago, her majesty's ministers were kind enough to send up for the convenience of members and to hang on the walls maps of our latest acquisitions and our "seats of war." We had maps of the Transvaal and of Cyprus and the harbors of Famagousta, Limasol, and all the rest of it. Then came "the seat of war" in Afghanistan, which covered all that remained of the wall, and the other day, when the clerks of the Intelligence Department came to fix up our newest "seat of war," it was discovered that we had on hand so many "seats of war" that there was no room on the wall for more.

If this is to go on, where is it to end? I will tell you that it will not end so long as her majesty's government can have money voted in this House on the excuse that because we are involved in war, money must be voted to carry it on. It is always too late or too soon to protest. For my part, I take my stand against what seems to have become a system of plunging us without our knowledge or concurrence into wars from which our consciences revolt, and then, because the butcher's bill is incurred, telling us government must needs have the money—that it would be "unpatriotic" to refuse it.

I know there are honorable members round about me who will say: "We are as much opposed to this Zulu war as any man can be. We believe it to be an unjust war, but will vote for the money because the country is now engaged in the struggle." I can quite recognize that

as a ground which some members of this House
may take up; far be it from me to quarrel
with them; but, for myself, I say my conscience
recoils from having act, hand, or part in voting
a sixpence for this war. I challenge any man
in or out of this House to defend it on the principles of public equity, if he will only suppose
that it is Russia that is waging the war, and not
England. I say no man in this House will dare
to apply to such a war the principles which you
apply elsewhere. If this dusky chief, spear in
hand, set forth to defend his home against the
Frank, the Russian, or the German, English pens
would trace his record of glory, and English
poets would sing his fame. We have had sym-
pathetically dramatized for us the story of Pizarro, when men—savages perhaps, but patriots all
the same—withstood the civilizing tyrant that
came upon their shores. And when we stand in
Pizarro's place in South Africa to-day, is no
voice to be raised in England better worthy of
being heard than mine to say, as I say now,
"This is an iniquitous and a wicked war; it is
against all my convictions of right and wrong?"

And at what an hour do we find ourselves so
far gone in this onward march of aggression,
this lust of territory, this greed of annexation?
It is at the very moment that you have been
contesting the right of a Christian power to redress Christian wrongs in the east of Europe.
You call Russia an aggressive power, and treat
us to homilies on the iniquity of her pushing

her frontiers forward. Was ever hypocrisy so gigantic as yours? To call Russia aggressive, when you are reaching out your hands to grasp more territory in every region of the globe, by every violation of right. It is incontestable that you led the Zulu king to conclude that you favored his claims to this strip of land. But no sooner had you annexed the Transvaal than you turn round upon him in conduct which he calls, and I say, justly calls, something very like perfidy. Now that you are the rulers of the Transvaal, you say he shall not have what you notoriously led him to expect as his just and lawful right.

Where slumbers the public morality of England? I look in vain in the public press of this country for that voice which ought to speak out, when we read the ultimatum—that impudent and insolent missive—of Sir Bartle Frere. I know of nothing more audacious than the document which was sent to provoke this war; yet now the land is agitated from end to end by the story of the terrible disaster at Isandlana, and money is being sought here to-night, not for defense of your South African possessions, but in order to wage a war of vengeance on Cetewayo and give up his people to sword and flame.

I pay my tribute to the gallantry and heroism of those British soldiers who fell beneath their flag. They served their queen and their colors well. But while I admire them, I more admire

the men, savages tho they be, who fell with
their feet on their native soil defending themselves against an invader. My morality is not
cribbed, cabined, and confined by geographical
lines. I mete out to the savage the same measure
of justice which I extend to more civilized races.
Altho a man be a savage, we ought not to deny
him the degree of praise which is due to his
patriotism, as praise is paid to Caractacus and
Kosciusko. This Zulu king stood within his
own territories. He only did what Queen Elizabeth did in the case of the Spanish Armada
when it threatened English soil. He called his
forces around him, as she did hers, and said:
"I will make the invader bite the dust." And
he did so.

England, with the £1,500,000 you vote to-
night, will doubtless succeed in a war of revenge
upon this African prince. £1,500,000! Why, if
the government had asked for £5,000,000 they
would have got it. If I saw Cetewayo pushing
his advantage so far as to invade the territories
which do not belong to him, and to endanger the
safety of peaceful settlers who are outside his
own land, I could sympathize with your military movements. But in so far as he stands in
the position of one who is resisting aggression,
and is on his own soil, defending his own people
and country, for my part I can not avoid con-
fessing—whatever consequences may follow from
my avowing it—that my sympathies are on his
side. I say he ought to have from us the same

admiration that the writers of history have taught us to pay to the men who resisted Spanish invaders in another clime.

I prize highly the advantages of civilization, and the blessings of civil and religious liberty; but never shall a vote of mine be given to encourage unjust invasion and conquest on the pretext of pushing "civilization," or to carry the Bible with the sword, so that rapacity may call its crimes "the diffusion of Christianity."

No, sir; I will give no vote to extend this already swollen empire at the cost of the liberty of these natives, howsoever dark their skin may be. I protest here to-night against further annexations. I believe if the representatives of Ireland, or the people of Ireland, had a voice in this question they would say that the British Empire is wide enough, great enough, grand enough, powerful enough, rich enough, without sending an ultimatum to take a rood of ground from Cetewayo. We might leave this dusky warrior to himself, and the British ensign would float as proudly from the turrets of Windsor Castle as it does now. Nay, much better and happier might we all be by giving up these aggressive enterprises and costly schemes of aggrandizement. It is while trade is languishing, and industries are perishing in our midst, and the cry of absolute destitution comes to us from the midland counties, £1,500,000 is being asked from us to carry out this most iniquitous business.

All vainly I speak. To-night this money will be voted. I know that well. But I know what verdict will yet be passed on this episode of British history. When the present feeling of resentment has passed away, when passion has cooled, and reason returned, there will arise some Allison, or some Macaulay, or some Lecky, to trace for our indignant posterity the story of this hour. They will say it was a reproach to the British Parliament that it had not patriotism enough or independence enough to resist and refuse this application for money to spend in a war which they will declare to be, as I declare it to be, as unjust, as wicked, and as wanton as that which George III. waged—thank God, he waged in vain!—against the liberty-loving people of the American Colonies.

PARNELL

I

ON THE FORGED LETTER PRINTED IN THE LONDON "TIMES"[1]

(1887)

Born in 1846, died in 1891; elected to Parliament in 1875; President of the Irish Land League in 1879; visited the United States in 1879; imprisoned under the Coercion Act, 1881; in alliance with Gladstone for Home Rule in 1886; recovered five thousand pounds damages from the London *Times* for libel in 1889.

IT appears that, in addition to the passage of this Coercion Act, the dice are to be loaded—that your great organs of public opinion in this country are to be permitted to pay miserable creatures for the purpose of producing these calumnies. Who will be safe in such circumstances and under such conditions? I do not envy the right honorable gentleman, the chief secretary for Ireland, this first commencement of suppression and defense—this first commencement of calumny and of forgery which has been made by his supporters.

Now, sir, when I first heard of this precious

[1] From a speech delivered in the House of Commons on April 18, 1887. The forged letter purporting to have been written by Parnell had been reproduced (on the same day) by the London *Times* in facsimile. The letter gave countenance to the Phœnix Park murders.

concoction—I heard of it before I saw it, because I do not take in or even read the *Times* usually—when I heard that a letter of this description, bearing my signature, had been published in the *Times,* I supposed that some autograph of mine had fallen into the hands of some person for whom it had not been intended, and that it had been made use of in this way.

I supposed that some blank sheet containing my signature, such as many members who are asked for their signature frequently send—I supposed that such a blank sheet had fallen into hands for which it had not been intended, and that it had been misused in this fashion, or that something of that kind had happened.

But when I saw what purported to be my signature, I saw plainly that it was an audacious and unblushing fabrication. Why, sir, many members of this House have seen my signature, and if they will compare it with what purports to be my signature in the *Times* of this morning they will see that there are only two letters in the whole name which bear any resemblance to letters in my own signature as I write it.

I can not understand how the conductors of a responsible, and what used to be a respectable, journal, could have been so hoodwinked, so hoaxed, so bamboozled, and that is the most charitable interpretation which I can place on it, as to publish such a production as that as my signature.

My writing—its whole character—is entirely different. I unfortunately write a very cramped hand; my letters huddle into each other, and I write with very great difficulty and slowness. It is, in fact, a labor and a toil to me to write anything at all. But the signature in question is written by a ready penman, who has evidently covered as many leagues of letter-paper in his life as I have yards.

Of course, this is not the time, as I have said, to enter into full details and minutæ as to comparisons of handwriting; but if the House could see my signature, and the forged, the fabricated signature, they would see that, except as regards two letters, the whole signature bears no resemblance to mine.

The same remark applies to the letter. The letter does not purport to be in my handwriting. We are not informed who has written it. It is not alleged even that it was written by anybody who was ever associated with me. The name of this anonymous letter-writer is not mentioned. I do not know who he can be. The writing is strange to me. I think I should insult myself if I said—I think, however, that I perhaps ought to say it, in order that my denial may be full and complete—that I certainly never heard of the letter.

I never directed such a letter to be written. I never saw such a letter before I saw it in the *Times* this morning. The subject-matter of the letter is preposterous on the surface. The

phraseology of it is absurd—as absurd as any
phraseology that could be attributed to me could
possibly be. In every part of it it bears absolute and irrefutable evidence of want of genuine-
ness and authenticity.

Politics are come to a pretty pass in this
country when a leader of a party of eighty-six
members has to stand up, at ten minutes past one,
in the House of Commons, in order to defend
himself from an anonymous fabrication such as
that which is contained in the *Times* of this
morning. I have always held, with regard to
the late Mr. Forster, that his treatment of his
political prisoners was a humane treatment, and
a fair treatment; and I think for that reason
alone, if for no other, he should have been
shielded from such an attempt as was made on
his life by the Invincible Association.

I never had the slightest notion in the world
that the life of the late Mr. Forster was in danger,
or that any conspiracy was on foot against him,
or any other official in Ireland or elsewhere. I
had no more notion than an unborn child that
there was such a conspiracy as that of the In-
vincibles in existence, and no one was more surprised, more thunderstruck, and more astonished
than I was when that bolt from the blue fell
upon us in the Phœnix Park murders.

I know not in what direction to look for this
calamity. It is no exaggeration to say that if I
had been in the park that day I would gladly
have stood between Lord Frederick Cavendish

and the daggers of the assassins, and, for the matter of that, between their daggers and Mr. Burke, too.

Now, sir, I leave this subject. I have suffered more than any other man from that terrible deed in the Phœnix Park, and the Irish nation has suffered more than any other nation through it.

You are going to plunge everything back into the seething caldron of disaffection. You can not see what the results of all this may be. We can only point to the experience of what has happened in past times. We anticipate nothing beneficial from this Bill, either to your country or to ours; and we should not be honest men if we did not warn you, with all the little force at our command, of the terrible dangers that may be before you.

I trust before this Bill goes into Committee, or at all events before it leaves Committee, the great English people will make their voices heard and impress upon their representatives that they must not go on any further with this coercive legislation.

If this House and its majority have not sense enough to see this the great heart of this country will see it, for I believe it is a great and generous heart that can sympathize even when a question is concerned in reference to which there have been so many political antipathies. I am convinced by what I have seen of the great meetings which have been held over the length and breadth of England and Scotland that the heart of your nation has been reached—that it has been touched, and tho our opponents may be in a majority to-day, that the real force of public opinion is not at their back.

A Bill which is supported by men, many of whom are looking over their shoulders and behind them, like the soldiers of an army which a panic is beginning to reach, to see which is their readiest mode of retreat, is not likely to get through the difficult times before it emerges from Committee. The result will be modifications of the provisions of the most drastic of the coercion acts ever introduced against Ireland since 1833.

Do not talk to me of comparing the suspension of the Habeas Corpus Act with the present Bill. We have suffered from both. We have suffered from some of the provisions of the present Bill, as well as from the Habeas Corpus Suspension Act, and we are able to compare the one with the other; and I tell you that the provisions of the Habeas Corpus Suspension Act empowered you to arrest and detain in prison those whom you suspected, but it guaranteed them humane treatment, which did much to soften the asperities that otherwise would have been bred between the two nations by that act. Your prisoners under the Habeas Corpus Act were not starved and tortured as they will be under this. Your political prisoners were not put upon a plank bed, and fed on sixteen ounces of bread and water per day, and compelled to pick oakum, and perform hard labor, as they will be under this Bill.

The Bill will be the means by which you will be enabled to subject your political prisoners to treatment in your jails which you reserve in England for the worst of criminals, and it is idle to talk about comparison with the suspension of the Habeas Corpus Act, under which your prisoners were humanely and properly treated—altho imprisonment is hard to bear under the best circumstances; but in the position in which this Bill will place them, your political prisoners will be deliberately starved with hunger and clammed with cold in your jails. I trust in God, sir, that this nation and this House may be saved from the degradation and the peril that the mistake of passing this Bill puts them in.

II

ON THE HOME RULE BILL [1]
(1886)

IF, Mr. Speaker, I intervene in the contest of giants which has been proceeding for so many days in this House in reference to this great question, it is not because I suppose that that intervention is specially suitable to the moment; and I certainly should not, under ordinary circumstances, have felt any self-confidence what-

[1] From his speech in the House of Commons June 7, 1886, on the second reading of the Government of Ireland Bill (*i.e.*, Home Rule Bill). Printed here by kind permission of the London *Times*.

ever in following so able and eloquent a member of this House as the right honorable gentleman, the member for the Eastern division of Edinburgh. But "Thrice is he armed who hath his quarrel just," and even a man so inferior from every point of view to the right honorable gentleman as I am, may hope upon this occasion not to be so much behind him as usual. The right honorable gentleman has sought—I think, very unfairly—to cast a lurid light upon the situation by an allusion to those unhappy outrages which have occurred in Kerry. I join the right honorable gentleman in expressing my contempt for these cowardly and disgraceful practises. I join him in that respect to the fullest extent.

Nor do I say that because for months evictions have been more numerous in Kerry than in all the rest of Munster taken together—neither do I say that that constitutes any excuse for these outrages, altho it may supply us with a reason for them; but when I denounce outrages I denounce them in all parts of Ireland, whether they occur in Ulster or in Kerry. But certainly I do condemn these outrages in Kerry; and the right honorable gentleman says very rightly that they must be put a stop to. Well, so say we all; but the right honorable gentleman would try to put a stop to them by resorting to the old bad method of coercion, which he and his friends have been using for the last eighty-six years, while we say with the prime minister: "Try the effect of self-government," and if Kerry men

then resort to outrages they will very soon find
that the rest of Ireland will put a stop to them.
Now, sir, the right honorable member for East
Edinburgh [Mr. Goschen] spoke about the
sovereignty of Parliament. I entirely agree
upon this point. We have always known since
the introduction of this Bill the difference between a coordinate and a subordinate Parliament, and we have recognized that the Legislature
which the prime minister proposes to constitute
is a subordinate Parliament—that it is not the
same as Grattan's Parliament, which was co-
equal with the Imperial Parliament, arising out
of the same Constitution given to the Irish people by the Crown, just in the same way, tho not
by the same means, as Parliamentary institutions were given to Great Britain by the sovereign. We understand this perfectly well. With
reference to the argument that has been used
against us, that I am precluded from accepting
this solution as a final solution because I have
claimed the restitution of Grattan's Parliament,
I would beg to say that I consider there are
practical advantages connected with the proposed statutory body, limited and subordinate to
this Imperial Parliament as it undoubtedly will
be, which will render it much more useful and
advantageous to the Irish people than was
Grattan's Parliament, and that the statutory
body which the right honorable gentleman proposes to constitute is much more likely to be a
final settlement than Grattan's Parliament.

We feel, therefore, that under this Bill this Imperial Parliament will have the ultimate supremacy and the ultimate sovereignty. I think the most useful part of the Bill is that in which the prime minister throws the responsibility upon the new Legislature of maintaining that order in Ireland without which no state and no society can exist. I understand the supremacy of the Imperial Parliament to be this—that they can interfere in the event of the powers which are conferred by this Bill being abused under certain circumstances. But the Nationalists in accepting this Bill go, as I think, under an honorable understanding not to abuse those powers; and we pledge ourselves in that respect for the Irish people, as far as we can pledge ourselves, not to abuse those powers, and to devote our energies and our influence which we may have with the Irish people to prevent those powers from being abused. But, if those powers should be abused, the Imperial Parliament will have at its command the force which it reserves to itself, and it will be ready to intervene, but only in the case of grave necessity arising.

I believe this is by far the best mode in which we can hope to settle this question. You will have real power of force in your hands, and you ought to have it; and if abuses are committed and injustice be perpetrated you will always be able to use that force to put a stop to them. You will have the power and the supremacy of Parliament untouched and unimpaired, just as tho this Bill had never been brought forward. We fully recognize this to be the effect of the Bill. I now repeat what I have already said on the first reading of the measure that we look upon the provisions of the Bill as a final settlement of this question, and that I believe that the Irish people have accepted it as such a settlement. We have had this measure accepted in the sense I have indicated by all the leaders of every section of national opinion both in Ireland and outside Ireland. It has been so accepted in the United States of America, and by the Irish population in that country with whose vengeance some honorable members are so fond of threatening us. Not a single dissentient voice has been raised against this Bill by any Irishman—not by any Irishman holding national opinions—and I need scarcely remind the House that there are sections among Irish Nationalists just as much as there are even among the great Conservative party. I say that as far as it is possible for a nation to accept a measure cheerfully, freely, gladly, and without reservation as a final settlement,—I say that the Irish people have shown that they have accepted this measure in that sense.

I will now leave this question of the supremacy of the Imperial Parliament, and I will turn to one that was strongly dwelt upon by the right honorable gentleman the member for East Edinburgh. I mean the influence which he fears the Irish priesthood will seek to exercise upon the future education of the Irish people. I may say at once that I am quite sure that the right honorable gentleman's apprehensions upon this subject are genuine, so far as they go, and that at the same time he has no desire to fan the flame of religious discord. On the whole, I think that the right honorable gentleman has spoken very fairly in reference to this part of the question; and I will not say that, perhaps as a Protestant, had I not had, as I have had, abundant experience of Ireland, I might not have been inclined to share his fears myself. Certainly, I have no such fears; but it is rather remarkable that this question of education is the only matter the right honorable gentleman has any fears about in dealing with the question of Protestant and Catholic in Ireland. I can, however, assure the right honorable gentleman that we Irishmen shall be able to settle this question of Irish education very well among ourselves. There are many Liberal Nationalists in Ireland—I call them Liberal Nationalists, because I take the phrase in reference to this question of education—there are many Liberal Nationalists who do not altogether share the views of the Roman Catholic Church upon the subject of education, and they are anxious that Ulster should remain an integral part of Ireland in order that they may share the responsibility of government and may influence that government by the feelings which they have with regard to this question of education. You may depend upon it that in an Irish Legislature Ulster, with such representatives as she now has in the Imperial Parliament, would be able to successfully resist the realization of any idea which the Roman Catholic hierarchy might entertain with regard to obtaining an undue control of Irish education. But I repeat that we shall be able to settle this question and others very satisfactorily to all the parties concerned among ourselves.

I observe that reticence has been exercised with regard to the financial question, of which such a point was made upon the first reading of the bill. The speech of the right honorable gentleman upon the first reading of the Bill undoubtedly produced a great sensation in the House and in this country. The right honorable gentleman, as I and others, and as I believe the country, understood him, argued on that occasion that Ulster was wealthier than either of the three other provinces, and that consequently the burden of taxation would chiefly fall upon her, and that without Ulster, therefore, it would be impossible to carry on the government of Ireland. The right honorable gentleman did not press the financial question very far to-day; but it would not be improper, perhaps, if we were to direct a little more of our attention to it. For instance, the great wealth of Ulster has been taken up as the war cry of the Loyal and Patriotic Union. The right honorable gentleman was not very fair in choosing the Income Tax, Schedule D, referring to trade and professions, as his standard and measure of the

relative wealth of the four provinces. The fair
measure of their relative wealth is their assess-
ment to the Income Tax under all the different
schedules, and also the value of the rateable
property in Ireland; and these tests show con-
clusively that, so far from Ulster being the
wealthiest of the four provinces—and the right
honorable gentleman does not deny it now—
Ulster comes third in point of relative wealth
per head of the population. She comes after
Leinster and Munster, and she is only superior
to impoverished Connaught.

I come next to the question of the protection
of the minority. I have incidentally dwelt on
this point in respect to the matter of education;
but I should like, with the permission of the
House, to say a few words more about it, because it is one on which great attention has been
bestowed. One would think from what we hear
that the Protestants of Ireland were going to be
handed over to the tender mercies of a set of
thugs and bandits. The honorable and gallant
member for North Armagh [Major Saunderson]
cheers that. I only wish that I was as safe in
the North of Ireland when I go there as the
honorable and gallant member would be in the
South. What do honorable gentlemen mean by
the protection of the loyal minority? In the
first place, I ask them what they mean by the
loyal minority. The right honorable member
for East Edinburgh [Mr. Goschen] does not
seem to have made up his mind, even at this late

stage of the discussion, as to what loyal Ulster he means. When asked the question, he said he meant the same loyal Ulster as was referred to by the prime minister in his speech; but he would not commit himself by telling us what signification he attributed to the prime minister's expression. Well, I have examined the prime minister's reference since then, and I find that he referred to the whole province of Ulster. He did not select a little bit of the province, because the opposition had not discovered this point at that time; and consequently I suppose I may assume that the right honorable member for East Edinburgh also referred to the whole province of Ulster when he asked for special protection for it. He has not, however, told us how he would specially protect it.

You must give up the idea of protecting the Protestants either as a body or as a majority by the establishment of a separate legislature either in Ulster or in any portion of Ulster. No, sir, we can not give up a single Irishman. We want the energy, the patriotism, the talents, and the work of every Irishman to insure that this great experiment shall be a successful one. We want, sir, all creeds and all classes in Ireland. We can not consent to look upon a single Irishman as not belonging to us.

We do not blame the small proportion of the Protestants of Ireland who feel any real fear. I admit, sir, that there is a small proportion of them who do feel this fear. We do not blame them; we have been doing our best to allay that fear, and we shall continue to do so. Theirs is not the shame and disgrace of this fear. That shame and disgrace belong to right honorable gentlemen and noble lords of English political parties who, for selfish interests, have sought to rekindle the embers—the almost expiring embers—of religious bigotry. Ireland has never injured the right honorable gentleman, the member for West Birmingham. I do not know why he should have added the strength of his powerful arm; why he should, like another Brennus—let us hope not with the same result— why he should have thrown his sword into the scale against Ireland. I am not aware that we have either personally or politically attempted to injure the right honorable gentleman, yet he and his kind seek to dash this cup from the lips of the Irish people—the first cup of cold water that has been offered to our nation since the recall of Lord Fitzwilliam.

The question of the retention of the Irish members I shall only touch upon very slightly. I have always desired to keep my mind thoroughly open upon it, and not to make it a vital question. There are difficulties, but they are rather more from the English than the Irish point of view, and I think that when we come to consider that question in Committee that feeling will be a growing one on the part of Liberal members. I admit the existence of a strong sentiment in favor of our retention. I will not say it is a reasonable sentiment, when I consider how many times my colleags and I have been forcibly ejected from this House, how often the necessity of suspending, if not entirely abrogating, representation on the part of Ireland has been eagerly canvassed by the London Press as the only necessary solution of it—perhaps I may not, under these circumstances, consider the desire on the part of Liberal members as a very reasonable one. I admit that it is an honest one. All I can say is that when the prime minister has produced his plan, without binding myself beforehand, I shall candidly examine it, with a desire not to see in it an element that will injure the permanency of the settlement.

Now, sir, what does it all come to? It comes to two alternatives when everything has been said and everything has been done. One alternative is the coercion which Lord Salisbury put before the country, and the other is the alternative offered by the prime minister, carrying with it the lasting settlement of a treaty of peace. If you reject this bill, Lord Salisbury was quite right in what he said as to coercion. With great respect to the cries of "No" by honorable members above the gangway, I beg to say, you will have to resort to coercion. That is not a threat on my part—I would do much to prevent the necessity for resorting to coercion; but I say it will be inevitable, and the best-intentioned Radical who sits on those benches, and who thinks that he "never, never will be a party to coercion," will be found very soon walking into the division lobby in favor of the strongest and most drastic coercion bill, or, at the very outside, pitifully abstaining. We have gone through it all before. During the last five years I know, sir, there have been very severe and drastic coercion bills; but it will require an even severer and more drastic measure of coercion now. You will require all that you have had during the last five years, and more besides.

What, sir, has that coercion been? You have had, sir, during those five years—I do not say this to influence passion or awaken bitter memories—you have had during those five years the suspension of the Habeas Corpus Act; you have had a thousand of your Irish fellow subjects held in prison without specific charge, many of them for long periods of time, some of them for twenty months, without trial and without any intention of placing them on trial—I think of all these thousand persons arrested under the Coercion Act of the late Mr. Forster scarcely a dozen were put on their trial; you have had the Arms Acts; you have had the suspension of trial by jury—all during the last five years. You have authorized your police to enter the domicile of a citizen, of your fellow subject in Ireland, at any hour of the day or night, and to search every part of this domicile, even the beds of the women, without warrant. You have fined the

innocent for offenses committed by the guilty;
you have taken power to expel aliens from this
country; you have revived the Curfew Law and
the blood-money of your Norman conquerors;
you have gagged the Press and seized and suppressed newspapers; you have manufactured
new crimes and offenses, and applied fresh penalties unknown to your laws for these crimes
and offenses. All this you have done for five
years, and all this and much more you will have
to do again. The provision in the bill for ter-
minating the representation of Irish members
has been very vehemently objected to, and the
right honorable gentleman, the member for the
Border Burghs [Mr. Trevelyan], has said that
there is no half-way house between separation
and the maintenance of law and order in Ireland
by imperial authority. I say, with just as much
sincerity of belief, and just as much experience
as the right honorable gentleman that, in my
judgment, there is no half-way house between
the concession of legislative autonomy to Ireland
and the disfranchisement of the country and her
government as a crown colony. But, sir, I refuse to believe that these evil days must come.
I am convinced there are a sufficient number of
wise and just members in this House to cause it
to disregard appeals made to passion and to
pocket, and to choose the better way of the
prime minister—the way of founding peace and
good will among nations; and when the numbers
in the division lobby come to be told, it will

also be told, for the admiration of all future generations, that England and her Parliament, in this nineteenth century, was wise enough, brave enough, and generous enough to close the strife of centuries, and to give peace, prosperity, and happiness to suffering Ireland.

MICHAEL DAVITT

ON THE IRISH LAND LEAGUE[1]
(1889)

Born in 1846, died in 1906; joined the Irish Movement in 1865; sentenced to penal servitude for treason and felony in 1870, and served seven and a half years; helped to found the Irish Land League in 1879; arrested and imprisoned for political offenses in 1881 and again in 1883; while in prison elected to Parliament but disqualified by vote of the House; reelected in 1892, but unseated; elected again in 1899.

I AM only too sensible of the fact that I have trespassed upon the patience and forbearance of the court to an extent which, possibly, would not be permitted to a lawyer. I am thankful, therefore, for such latitude, as well as for the unfailing fairness and courtesy of your lordships toward me personally from the very commencement of this inquiry.

I know too well I have spoken hot words and resorted to hard phrases in arguments, which may have been out of place in the calm region of a court like this. But that was because I felt that the character of the charges I have tried to meet and to answer was such as merited the strongest possible language of condemnation. I came here to address this court contrary to the advice of Mr. Parnell, who was the central figure

[1] From a speech delivered before the Special Irish Commission in October, 1889. By kind permission of Messrs. Kegan, Paul, Trench, Trubner & Co.

and chief object of the *Times's* malignant allegations.

I have, therefore, spoken only for myself. I felt that it was my duty to come here, no matter who should advise me to the contrary. I may be wrong in my opinion, but I thought and believed that if one with my record of suffering, physical and otherwise, at the hands of Irish landlordism and Castle rule; of the conflict of a lifetime with the law as it has been administered in Ireland, and of the punishment which that conflict has entailed: I felt and believed if I came before this tribunal and pleaded, in my own way, the cause of the Celtic peasantry of Ireland, that perhaps the story which I have told and the case which I have submitted might possibly, in part or in whole, arrest the attention of the people of Great Britain when they come to study your lordships' labors and report.

And I thought and hoped that in the defense which I have made there might possibly be found some help in the task of finally solving this Anglo-Irish struggle. Should my hope be realized, should I have contributed but in the least possible degree to point to a just and feasible solution of a problem which would bring peace and some chance of prosperity to Ireland, I shall be happy in the recollection of the task which I am now bringing to a close.

I can only say that I represent the working classes of my country here as I did in the Land League movement, and I know they feel, as I do, that, no matter how bitter past memories have rankled in our hearts, no matter how much we have suffered in the past in person or in our country's cause, no matter how fiercely some of us have fought against and denounced the injustice of alien misgovernment: I know that, before a feeling of kindness and of good will on the part of the people of England, Scotland, and Wales, and in a belief in their awakening sense of justice toward our country, all distrust and opposition and bitter recollections will die out of the Irish heart, and the Anglo-Irish strife will terminate forever when landlordism and Castle rule are dethroned by Great Britain's verdict for reason and for right.

My lords, I now bring my observations to a close. Whatever legal points are to occupy your lordships' study and care in this long and arduous investigation, it will appear to the public, who will study the report or the decision of this tribunal, that two institutions stood indicted before it.

One has had a life of centuries, the other an existence of but a few brief years. They are charged, respectively, by the accused and the accusers, with the responsibility for the agrarian crimes of the period covered by this inquiry.

One is Irish landlordism, the other is the Irish Land League. The *Times* alleges that the younger institution is the culprit. The Land League, through me, its founder, repels the accusation, and countercharges landlordism with being the instigation and the cause, not alone of the agrarian violence and crimes from 1879 to 1887, but of all which are on record, from the times spoken of by Spenser and Davis in the days of Elizabeth down to the date of this Commission.

To prove this real and hoary-headed culprit guilty I have not employed or purchased the venal talent of a forger, or offered the tempting price of liberty for incriminatory evidence to unhappy convicts in penal cells. Neither have I brought convicted assassins or professional perjurers, like the Delaneys and Le Carons, before your lordships. I have not sought assistance such as this with which to sustain my case. Nor have I been aided by the Colemans, Buckleys, and Igos as confederates, or had to scour the purlieus of American cities for men who would sell evidence that might repair the case which Richard Pigott's confession destroyed, and which his self-inflicted death has sealed with tragic emphasis.

But there is another and a higher interest involved in the drama of this Commission now rapidly drawing to a close; an interest far surpassing in importance, and the possible consequences of your lordships' judgment, anything else comprised in this investigation. It stands between the *Times* and landlordism on the one hand; the persons here charged and the Land League on the other. In bygone ages historians, with some prophetic instinct, called it "The Isle of Destiny."

And Destiny seems to have reserved it for a career of trial, of suffering, and of sorrow. That same Destiny has linked this country close to England. Politically it has remained there for seven hundred years or more. During that period few people ever placed upon this earth have experienced more injustice or more criminal neglect at the hands of their rulers than we have.

This even English history will not and dare not deny. This land so tried and treated has nevertheless struggled, generation after generation, now with one means, now with another, to widen the sphere of its contracted religious, social, and political liberties—liberties so contracted by the deliberate policy of its English governing power; and ever and always were these struggles made against the prejudice and might, and often the cruelties, of this same power, backed by the support or the indifference of the British nation.

But despite all this the cause so fought and upheld has ever and always succeeded, sooner or later, in vindicating its underlying principles of truth and justice, and in winning from the power which failed to crush them an after-justification of their righteous demands.

A people so persevering in its fight for the most priceless and most cherished of human and civil rights, so opposed, but so invariably vindicated, might surely in these days of progress and of enlightenment excite in the breasts of Englishmen other feelings than those of jealousy, hate, revenge, and fear. To many, thank God, it has appealed successfully at last to what is good and what is best in English nature. It has spoken to the spirit of Liberty, and has turned the love of justice in the popular mind toward Ireland, and has asked the British people, in the interests of peace, to put force and mistrust away with every other abandoned weapon of Ireland's past misrule, and to place in their stead the soothing and healing remedies of confidence and friendship, based upon reason and equality.

But one thing, at least, the history of this commission will have to tell to future generations. It will narrate how this progress of conciliation between ruled and rulers was sought to be arrested; how a people asking for justice were answered by ferocious animosity; how men who had suffered imprisonment, degradation, and calumny in their country's service were foully attacked by the weapons of moral assassination, and how every dastard means known in the records of political warfare was purchased and employed to cripple or destroy the elected representative of the Irish nation.

This story will picture this once-powerful organ of English public opinion earning again the title of "literary assassin" which Richard Cobden gave it near thirty years ago. It will stand again in this light when its writers are seen plotting with Houston, planning with Pigott, and bargaining with Delaney how best to reawaken in the English mind the old hate and jealousy and fear of a people who were to be depicted in its columns in the most odious and repulsive character that forgers' or libelers' mercenary talent could delineate in "Parnellism and Crime."

This story will exhibit these men sitting in the editorial rooms of Printing House Square, with professions of loyalty on their lips and poison in their pens; with "honesty" loudly proclaimed in articles which salaried falsehood had written; with simulated regard for truth, making "Shame ashamed" of their concocted fabrications.

And these men, with the salaries of the rich in their pockets and the smiles of London society as their reward, now carry on a deliberately planned system of infamous allegation against political opponents who were but striving to redeem the sad fortunes of their country in efforts to bring to an end a strife of centuries' duration between neighboring nations and peoples.

Between the *Times* on the one hand, and the accused on the other, your lordships are, however, first to judge. It is, if I may say so without presumption, as serious and momentous a duty as judges of England were ever called upon to perform. The traditions of your lordships' exalted position, elevated as that position is above the play of political passion, of the influence of fear or favor, will call, and will not, I am sure, call in vain, for the exercise of all those great qualities of trained ability, of calmness, of discernment, of judgment, and of courage which are the proud boast of the judicial bench of this land.

Whether or not the test of a cold, indiscriminating law will alone decide an issue in which political passion has played so great a part, and where party feeling has been a moving principle in acts and words; whether the heated language of platform oratory, or the sometimes crude attempts of political reform, are to be weighed in the balance of legal scales—scales never fashioned, at least in England, to measure the bounds of political action; or whether the test is to lie with a discriminating judicial amalgam of law in its highest attributes and of calm reason applied to the men and motives and means of the Land League, as the accused, and to the *Times,* its charges and allegations, as the accuser, I am, as a layman, unable to forecast.

But, be the test what it may, if it be only based upon truth and guided by the simple monitor of common sense, I say on my own behalf and on that of the Land League and of the peasantry of Ireland, hopefully, confidently, fearlessly, "Let justice be done tho the heavens fall."

JOHN DILLON

ON THE DEATH OF GLADSTONE[1]

(1898)

Born in 1851; one of the leaders of the Irish Nationalist party; entered Parliament as a Parnellite in 1880; reelected in 1892, 1895, 1897, and 1900; imprisoned in 1881-82 and again in 1891; became Chairman of the Irish Nationalist party in 1896.

As an Irishman I feel that I have a special right to join in paying a tribute to the great Englishman who died yesterday, because the last and, as all men will agree, the most glorious years of his strenuous and splendid life were dominated by the love which he bore to our nation, and by the eager and even passionate desire to serve Ireland and give her liberty and peace. By virtue of the splendid quality of his nature, which seemed to give him perpetual youth, Mr. Gladstone's faith in a cause to which he had once devoted himself never wavered, nor did his enthusiasm grow cold. Difficulties and the weight of advancing years were alike ineffectual to blunt the edge of his purpose or to daunt his splendid courage, and even when racked with pain, and when the shadow of death was darkening over him, his heart still yearned toward the people of Ireland, and his last public utterance

[1] Delivered in the House of Commons May 20, 1898. Printed here by kind permission of the London *Times*.

was a message of sympathy for Ireland and of hope for her future.

His was a great and deep nature. He loved the people with a wise and persevering love. His love of the people and his abiding faith in the efficacy of liberty and of government based on the consent of the people, as an instrument of human progress, was not the outcome of youthful enthusiasm, but the deep-rooted growth of long years, and drew its vigor from an almost unparalleled experience of men and of affairs. Above all men I have ever known or read of, in his case the lapse of years seemed to have no influence to narrow his sympathies or to contract his heart. Young men felt old beside him. And to the last no generous cause, no suffering people, appealed to him in vain, and that glorious voice which had so often inspirited the friends of freedom and guided them to victory was to the last at the service of the weak and the oppressed of whatever race or nation. Mr. Gladstone was the greatest Englishman of his time.

He loved his own people as much as any Englishman that ever lived. But through communion with the hearts of his own people he acquired that wider and greater gift—the power of understanding and sympathizing with other peoples. He entered into their sorrows and felt for their oppressions. And with splendid courage he did not hesitate, even in the case of his much-loved England, to condemn her when he thought she was wronging others, and in so doing he fearlessly faced odium and unpopularity among his own people, which it must have been bitter for him to bear; and so he became something far greater than a British statesman, and took a place amid the greatest leaders of the human race. Amid the obstructions and the cynicism of a materialistic age he never lost his hold on the "ideal." And so it came to pass that wherever throughout the civilized world a race or nation of men were suffering from oppression, their thoughts turned toward Gladstone, and when that mighty voice was raised in their behalf Europe and the civilized world listened, and the breathing of new hopes entered into the hearts of men made desperate by long despair.

In the years that have gone by England has lost many men who served their country splendidly and round whose graves the British people deeply mourned; but round the death-bed of Gladstone the people of this island are joined in their sorrow by many peoples, and to-day throughout the Christian world—in many lands and in many tongues—prayers will be offered to that God on whom in his last supreme hour of trial Mr. Gladstone humbly placed his firm reliance, begging that He will remember to His great servant how ardently he loved his fellow men, without distinction of race, while he lived among them, and how mightily he labored for their good.

JOHN E. REDMOND

IRELAND AND THE CORONATION [1]
(1902)

Born in 1851; entered Parliament in 1876; became an organizer of
the Home Rule Movement; adhered to Parnell during the break in
the Nationalist party; succeeded John Dillon as head of the party
when reorganized in 1900.

GENTLEMEN, the event which is being celebrated
to-day in London is one of great historic signifi-
cance and importance. The monarch of this
mighty Empire is being crowned, and there are
assembled in London representatives from all
parts of the Empire to acclaim Edward VII. as
the constitutional monarch of these realms. There
is only one absentee—Ireland. Gentlemen, in
Ireland Edward VII. is not a constitutional
monarch. No English sovereign has been a constitutional monarch of Ireland since the Union,
and to-day the Nationalist representatives of Ireland renew the protest—which has never been al-
lowed to die for one hundred years—against the
destruction of our Constitution and the usurpation of the government of our country by England.

Now, we claim that Ireland is not bound,
morally or legally, by any laws which are not

[1] From a speech delivered in the City Hall, Dublin, August 9,
1902, while Edward VII. was being crowned in London. From a
copy furnished for this collection by Mr. Redmond.

made by the Sovereign, Lords and Commons of
Ireland. We specifically deny the moral or
legal and constitutional right of the English
Parliament to legislate for Ireland. Upon what
does this claim rest? The Irish Parliament—
people certainly in England seem quite oblivious
of the fact—the Irish Parliament was almost
coeval with and absolutely coordinate with the
Parliament of England, and the first Irish Parliament of which we have any authentic records
sat in 1295, and from 1295 until 1495 that Parliament was absolutely supreme, a sovereign
Parliament, and no law made in England was
binding in Ireland, and altho in 1495 what was
known as Poyning's Law was passed, which provided that the heads of all bills to be introduced
into the Irish Parliament were first to be ap-
proved by the king and privy council of England, still that law was an Irish law passed by an
Irish Parliament, and did not sacrifice the inde-
dependence of the Irish Parliament or recognize
England's right to make laws for Ireland. It
reserved a coordinate authority with the English Parliament, and this condition remained un-
broken—aye, remained unquestioned until the
reign of George I., and then, in 1719, an English
Act was passed declaring that the English Parliament had power of making laws for Ireland.

Now, that clause was always resisted by this
country. Ireland never for one hour ceased to
protest against it, until at last, in 1782, the freedom of the Irish Parliament was obtained by

the great measure which Grattan, backed by the Irish Volunteers, passed into law. The act of George I. was repealed, and the English act of the 23d of George III., chapter 28, solemnly declared as follows: ''Be it enacted that the right claimed by the people of Ireland to be bound only by laws enacted by his majesty and the Parliament of that kingdom in all cases whatsoever, shall be, and is hereby declared and ascertained for ever, and shall at no time hereafter be questioned or questionable.'' Well, we know that eighteen years after that solemn declaration it was disregarded, and the Irish Parliament, which lasted for five hundred years, was destroyed by the Act of Union. Gentlemen, the Act of Union was carried by force and fraud, by treachery and falsehood. Speaking to an ordinary Irish audience it is unnecessary for me to labor these facts, but I hope you will forgive me if I attempt, in a few observations, to place our case upon record just as if we were making our case to England and not speaking here upon Irish soil. Mr. Lecky, in the second volume of his history, says: ''The sacrifice of nationality was extorted by the most enormous corruption in the history of representative institutions. It was demanded by no considerable portion of the Irish people; it was effected without a dissolution, in opposition to the universal majority of the representatives of the counties and considerable towns, and to innumerable addresses from all parts of the country. The Union was a crime of deepest turpitude, which, by imposing with every circumstance of infamy a new form of government on a reluctant and protesting nation, has vitiated the whole cause of Irish opinion." Lord Grey, speaking after the Union, in England, pointed out there were 300 members in the Irish Parliament. Of that number 120 members strongly opposed the Union, and 162 voted in favor of it; and of those 162, 116 were placemen in the pay of the English government.

Now, from that day to this, Ireland has never ceased to protest against the usurpation of the government of Ireland by the English Parliament. She has never ceased to protest according to the circumstances and the opportunities of the moment. She has protested by means of armed insurrections, and generation after generation has witnessed brave and gallant men sacrificing their lives in prison cell or on the scaffold in defense of Irish freedom. She has protested against it by agitation—never-ceasing agitation—protested against it from generation to generation, on the floor of the foreign assembly to which the Irish representatives have been sent. It is quite true that Ireland has from time to time been willing to compromise her claim for the restoration of Gratton's Coordinate Parliament. For example, she was willing in the days of Isaac Butt to accept a place in a federal union. She was willing in the time of Parnell to accept such a settlement as Gladstone offered. And I say here to-day—and I claim that I am entitled to speak on this point with authority—I claim to-day that Ireland and the Irish party stand on this question precisely where Parnell stood in '86. Altho that is so, Ireland has always denied and Ireland still denies that the Union was binding upon her either legally or morally. And here on this historic occasion we have assembled to renew our protest and to place it upon record.

Well, England thus destroyed our Constitution in 1800. What has she given us in return? Has she given us in return her own Constitution? Nothing of the kind. Never for one single hour since the Union was passed has Ireland been a constitutionally governed country. Never for one hour has the sovereign of England been the constitutional sovereign of Ireland. Ireland, in effect, has since 1800 been governed as a Crown Colony, with certain empty forms and pretenses of constitutionalism. Never for one hour has the English government of Ireland obtained the assent, or approval, or confidence of the people of Ireland. Never for one hour have the elected representatives of the majority of the Irish people had the control or even a potent voice in the government of this country. Never for one hour since then has the English government of Ireland rested upon anything except naked force and unabashed corruption. Never for one hour has the British Constitution been in force in this country, whose own Constitution was destroyed. Why, the mere fact that in one hundred years, eighty-seven coercion acts have been passed by the English Parliament for Ireland, in spite of Irish protest, is sufficient to establish the facts that I have adduced. Martial law, suspension of the Habeas Corpus Act, suspension of trial by jury, suppression of free speech—these have been the permanent blessings conferred on Ireland by the destruction of the Irish Constitution. No single reform, large or small, has ever been obtained by purely constitutional methods. Let any Englishman who questions that answer this question: Let him point to any single act of justice or reform which has not been extorted in one way or another from the British Parliament by force or by fear. Catholic emancipation, falsely promised before the Union, granted, in the words of Wellington, to avoid civil war. The Church Act and the Land Act, produced by the influence of Fenianism.

Allow me for a moment to turn to another aspect of our case. The suppression of the Constitution in Ireland has been followed by disasters unparalleled in the history of the world. Under English rule millions of our people have died by artificial famines, and hundreds of thousands of homes have been leveled by the crowbar brigade. People talk of the devastation in the Transvaal and Orange River Free State. Horrible, inhuman, and disgraceful as that was, it was as nothing compared to what happened in Ireland under the so-called constitutional rule of the English Parliament. The Transvaal, after all, was in a state of war. But in Ireland, in a state of peace, the homes of the people have been leveled, the population of our country has been largely exterminated or expatriated, and our fair and smiling fields have been laid waste and desolate. People sometimes speak of famine as an act of God—an impious phrase, in my opinion, never true in any time or country, but in Ireland the phrase is absolute blasphemy. The Irish famine has been the direct result of English misgovernment.

After all, Ireland, taken as a whole, is a rich and fertile island. With a proper distribution of the population, and with the fostering care of a native government, a population of many millions more than the present ought to live in our land in comfort and happiness. And yet it has marked every part of the rule of Ireland by the English Parliament. In one great visitation half a century ago a million and a quarter of our people died by starvation in the midst of a country which was actually at that time exporting food and grain to the English markets, and which was all the time paying exorbitant rates to maintain the glory and the power of the British Empire. In 1849 there was a Parliamentary return issued, from which it appears that during the three famine years ending in January, 1849, Ireland paid in taxes to the British exchequer £13,293,681—and her starving people perished of starvation in hundreds and thousands by the roadside—exported to England 500,000 head of cattle, 1,000,000 sheep, 500,000 pigs, 1,000,000 quarters of wheat-flour, 3,500,000 quarters of oats and meal. Good God, what a picture! Here is a country paying millions of pounds in taxation to maintain the glory of the Empire to which it is allied, a country exporting millions of beasts and millions of quarters of grain out of the country, and all the time hundreds of thousands of people dying of starvation by the roadside.

Gentlemen, from that day to this the population of our country has gone steadily down from 8,500,000 men to 4,500,000 now. In the reign of Queen Victoria 1,225,000 people died of starvation, 4,000,000 people during that reign were evicted, 4,800,000 people emigrated from the shores of our country, and it is still going on. People who come to this country and pay flying visits to the West of Ireland and see some of the congested districts go away with the idea that Ireland is all a barren mountain or bog. Yes, the congested districts are poor; but the real secret of the position is that the richer parts of Ireland have been made desolate, have been depopulated, and turned into mere cattle ranches.

Fraud, robbery, and murder have characterized the English usurpation of the government of our country. Why, for the last fifty years we have been robbed in the matter of taxes of hundreds of millions. Just in a sentence let me point this out. The accusation is made against England that she is robbing this country by unjust taxation. A tribunal is appointed to consider the question. Appointed by whom? Appointed by the accused, packed by the accused, a tribunal with a majority of Britishers on it, appointed by the accused person, and when the verdict is brought in in favor of Ireland that verdict is thrown in the waste-paper basket, and the English Empire proceeds complacently along, piling up year after year the taxes of this country, until to-day it is absolutely true that Ireland's contribution toward the expenses of the empire have been since that commission sat increased by almost £2,000,000 a year. We pay for the navy, and we have no commerce for the navy to protect; we pay for the army, and we loathe and execrate the work upon which it has been engaged.

And we hear English statesmen asking us why Ireland is not loyal. Lord Rosebery, the other day, declared that if Ireland were only loyal he would be willing to confer upon her a colonial constitution. Loyal—loyal to what? Why, there is no race in the world which, I believe, by instinct is more inclined to sentiments of loyalty than the Irish. Why do not these English statesmen give us something to be loyal to? What claim has such a system as that to loyalty? Grattan said that loyalty without liberty was corruption. What public liberty exists in Ireland to-day? The Constitution is suspended. The most trusted and honored men throughout the length and breadth of Ireland are being sent as common criminals to English jails on vague charges of conspiracy, sent there by degraded tribunals consisting of paid and removable servants of the man who brings the accusation. In Ireland there is neither liberty, prosperity, nor loyalty. There is oppression and poverty and misgovernment, and deep-seated and justifiable disloyalty, and to-day—if I may take it upon myself to speak the voice of this party on this historic occasion—I say to England in our names, "You may proceed with your coronation jubilations and celebrations, you may assemble all the nations of the world in London to witness an exhibition of the loyalty, and what you call the unity of the empire, but you can not hide from your guests the skeleton at your feast. You can not disguise from the world that one portion of that empire—and a portion which, all things considered, had probably as great a part in building up that empire as England itself—a portion which was the home of a brave and noble race which has spread throughout the world the fame of their talents, their virtues, and their valor—here lies at your very heart oppressed, impoverished, manacled, and disloyal, a reproach to your civilization, and a disgrace to your name. For these reasons, gentlemen, we, as a party, have decided to take no part in these celebrations.

END OF VOL. VI